Ex Libris

A gift from:

Harry Walker

In Memoriam:

Arthur S. Hecker

The World
of the Economist

"I think our boy's going to turn out all right."

THE
WORLD
OF THE
ECONOMI$T

Hugh S. Norton

University of South Carolina Press
Columbia, South Carolina

Library of Congress Cataloging in Publication Data

Norton, Hugh Stanton, 1921–
  The world of the economist.

  Bibliography: p.
  1. Economists, American. I. Title.
HB119.A3N6   330'.0973   73–7819
ISBN 0–87249–273–7

97657

Contents

Tables

Preface

WHO are the economists? One hears much about them. They advise the president of the United States. They forecast trends in the economy upon which important decisions are based. They are authors of popular books and seem to be increasingly influential. Yet the total number of professional economists in the U.S. is probably only about fifteen thousand, less than one-tenth the number of lawyers and about half the number of psychologists.

The average American, though he seldom knows an economist personally, is very much influenced by what they do, what they say and write, and how they think. The layman is apt to have professional contact with physicians, lawyers, and certain other professionals; and these professions have been the object of widespread interest—books, plays, and television serials revolve about them. The professional economist, in contrast, plys his trade behind the scenes. As teacher, adviser, or analyst, his work is apt to be impersonal. He is, in fact, akin to the geologist, physicist, statistician, or other scientists about whom the general public is only dimly aware.

The growing influence of economists, especially in government, coupled with their increasing appearance in the mass media has created interest in the profession both from students and from the general public. Who are these people? What constitutes their training? How much influence do they really have?

Economists are highly concentrated in a few fields of activity. About 45 percent are employed in higher education, and two other activities, business and government service, account for most of the rest.

This book explores the world of the professional economist—his training, his work, his philosophy, and recent changes in the outlook and future of the profession. Chapter 1 describes the basic outlines of the profession and in general terms sketches a profile of the economist. Chapter 2 deals with the philosophy of the economist and the field of economics as a science. Chapter 3 is devoted to the major activity of the professional economist, college and university teaching. For many years almost all economists were in this field, but by the mid-1930s they had begun to enter government in large numbers. Their participation in this area is described in Chapter 4. Most recently business has attracted the interest and talents of the professional economist. His function in the business world is considered in Chapter 5. Chapter 6 evaluates the social role of the economist and concludes the study.

The World of the Economist draws on and expands the work in two of the author's earlier publications, *The Role of the Economist in Government Policy Making* and *The Professional Economist: His Role in Business and Industry,* and is designed to inform the layman about the profession.

Many of my fellow economists have given me the benefit of their views and experiences. I am indebted to my colleagues at the University of South Carolina, Professors James L. Cochrane, B. F. Kiker, and Alfred G. Smith, Jr., all of whom read portions of the manuscript and made helpful comments, and to Professor E. Ray Canterbery of Florida State University who made major suggestions for improvement. Likewise, I am grateful to my typists, Mrs. Shirley T. Craft and Mrs. Evyette Goff, and as always to my wife and family for their consistent encouragement.

Hugh S. Norton

Columbia, South Carolina
May 15, 1973

*The World
of the Economist*

1
An Overview
of the Profession

THIS book deals with the professional economist as he carries on three major activities—college teaching, government service, and employment as economist in the business firm.

Although there are relatively few economists in the United States (only about as many as there are students in a medium size university), they have become a significant force in the nation's life. One reads daily about price changes, expectations of business investments, forecasts by the president's Council of Economic Advisers and other matters which constitute the economists' output. Will there be a major recession? Will the cost of living rise? Will unemployment increase during the year? Economists are not always able to answer these questions with great precision, but they can often make reasonable predictions and sometimes can help to determine the course of economic events. Their work is becoming increasingly useful to policy makers in both business and government.

Economists work with data concerning the economic system and are employed by banks, insurance companies, automobile manufacturers, and brokerage houses. Members of the Council of Economic Advisers counsel the president of the United States on economic matters while other economists advise officials at every level of government. Yet almost half of all professional economists are still found in colleges and universities, teaching economics or engaging in economic research and writing. In fact, the emergence of the economist on the national level has been of recent origin. Scarcely thirty years ago only a small number of economists were found in government and hardly any had appeared in the world of business.

Economics is a complex social science which generally requires a high level of formal education. Of course, many people who have an interest in economics or who study economic problems are not professional economists by training in any modern sense. Most professions become more formal in structure as time passes, and economics is no exception.

It Began with Adam

Adam Smith (1723–1790), is often thought of as the founder of the science. Smith, a professor of moral sciences at Glasgow, is perhaps best remembered for his landmark work, *An Inquiry into the Nature and Causes of the Wealth of Nations.* Just as Smith would find a modern economics curriculum strange and likely distasteful, modern students would find his book old fashioned. Until the early twentieth century academic economics was most often a blend of philosophy, history, political science, and mathematics and had little formal structure of its own. Economics generally was presented in academic form as political economy, and its practitioners had diverse backgrounds.

George Stigler has noted that the science of economics has become more professional with the passage of time, and in a stimulating essay he has traced the rise of professionalism, with the displacement of the amateur economist by the trained professional.[1] Stigler points out that much economic writing in England during the latter part of the eighteenth and early nineteenth centuries was done by nonprofessionals. Indeed, the literature of the period was dominated by nonprofessional writers who derived financial support from such professions as law and business or who were gentlemen scholars of independent means.[2]

Much the same situation prevailed in the United States. A great deal of economic writing was done by men who were neither trained in economics nor dependent upon its practice for their livelihood.

[1] *Essays in the History of Economics* (Chicago: University of Chicago Press, 1965), pp. 31–50.
[2] Stigler presents in tabular form occupational and other data about fifty-six important English economists (1766 to 1915). The list is heavy with journalists, clergymen, lawyers, engineers, soldiers, and gentlemen.

For some reason, medical men, newspapermen, printers, old soldiers, and engineers often interested themselves in the field.

Of the early American laymen, perhaps the most widely influential example was Henry George, a printer and journalist who died in 1897. George championed the single tax, and his famous book, *Progress and Poverty*, published in 1879, was read by and influenced a wide audience. However, George was not content to scribble in a garret and entered public life, running (without success) for mayor of New York City.

Even now a number of pamphleteers publish tracts on various economic subjects, among which gold, silver, and other monetary matters seem to be the most popular. Such lay writers have little currency in the profession. Although these writers often espouse unorthodox ideas, they now usually have sound professional credentials. The last major stand by the nonprofessionals took place in the troubled 1930s, when economic issues were in the forefront of everyone's mind. Nonprofessionals had a substantial following, and no account of the development of the economist's influence would be complete without some mention of these quasi economists who far outstripped the professionals in offering popular solutions for the nation's economic woes (not that this was hard to do).

Among the more easily classifiable quasi economists were those of the moderate left, socialists including the onetime governor of Minnesota Floyd Olson, the novelist Upton Sinclair with his End Poverty in California (EPIC) program, the doctrinaire communists, and such rightists as Seward Collins, Lawrence Dennis, and William Dudley Pelley. But the more popular of these messiahs do not fit easily into conventional categories. For instance, Senator Huey P. Long of Louisiana promoted the organization of a Share-the-Wealth Society, with the object (means were only vaguely hinted at) of providing each American family with an income of not less than $5,000 a year.[3]

Theories were advanced by other quasi economists, including F. E. Townsend, a retired California physician who originated the Townsend Pension Plan. Extremely popular among elderly citizens, this plan would have disbursed the revenues from a 2 percent federal

[3] One must note that in 1970 suggestions of a "negative income tax" or minimum incomes still fell far short of $5,000. In 1935, when Long was at his peak, $5,000 per year was considered to be affluent indeed.

transaction tax to people over sixty who would agree to quit work and spend the $200 a month dole as rapidly as it was received. A Michigan priest, Charles E. Coughlin, established a National Union for Social Justice, and under its auspices he advanced his monetary theories each week over a large, national radio network. Yet another plan was promoted by an engineer, Howard Scott, who advanced Technocracy, a specific, comprehensive alternative to free-enterprise capitalism based loosely on the theories of the economist Thorstein Veblen. An offshoot of this school advocated that the money supply be tied to the output of electric power as an index of economic activity.[4]

These movements attracted a number of followers, and although their political significance was not great, the Roosevelt administration was for a time forced to follow a policy of accommodation toward both Long and Coughlin. Although they were "unscientific," these economists were far ahead of their conventional associates in their advocacy of social welfare measures.

In the election of 1932 the combined strength of the various splinter groups was not impressive. Their intellectual appeal was apparently wider than their political appeal. It is hard to say how many people really understood the technical aspects of the Townsend Plan or the intricate workings of Technocracy, but it seems likely that there were relatively few, and most voted to stick with conventional capitalism.[5]

Although by 1900 academic economists were generally well and systematically trained, the same could not be said of their counterparts on the popular lecture circuit or in government. Academic economists, of course, dominated the profession, but they made little effort to extend their influence into the nonacademic world.

As in most professions, continued development tends to exclude those who lack formal training. At the same time the profession is increasingly influenced by those who do meet formal standards. In most cases, "formal standards" means formal academic training. Such standards widen the gulf between the professional and the layman. The professional acquires a jargon and a patina of learning from the "standard" works which separate him from the self-taught.

[4] In 1970, Coughlin was still alive, although he had abandoned his public career.

[5] The Socialist and Communist parties combined received 987,772 votes, FDR 22,821,857, and Hoover 15,761,841.

Despite these developments, economists who have slim professional credentials continue to wield substantial influence. It is difficult, for example, to place a popular, current economic writer such as Sylvia Porter.[6] These highly successful writers have wide followings, conduct columns or newsletters relating to economic affairs, and probably have a great influence, especially on the course of stock market operations. One has the impression that Miss Porter, for example, is especially influential among women investors. W. M. Kiplinger, perhaps the pioneer in the Washington "newsletter" field, was a former newsman who recognized the financial advantage of providing such a service and has been widely emulated. Kiplinger referred to himself as an economist although he had no formal training as such. Obviously, many popular economic writers would not be classified as professionals, but no doubt they would be unhappy to be excluded.

Thus we see at once that the professional economist is difficult to define. Unlike highly structured fields such as medicine in which practitioners are trained and licensed, many people who work in economics or call themselves economists do not conform to any fixed background and have no recognized training. Clearly, if we are to say much about the economist we must formulate some working definition. Not everyone would agree with the definition which follows, but it is widely used and seems to be reasonable.

Will the Real Economist Please Stand Up?

The professional economist is defined for the present purpose as one who: (1) is engaged in the full-time occupation of teaching economics on the college level, conducting economic studies, advising on economic matters, or performing economic analysis for business or government; (2) has professional economic training on the graduate level; and (3) is identifiable as a member of such professional groups as the American Economic Association or the National Association of Business Economists.[7]

According to the National Science Foundation definition, there

[6] Miss Porter's entry in *Who's Who* indicates that she received a bachelor's degree from Hunter College and did some graduate work at New York University. She holds many honorary degrees.

[7] This definition is somewhat similar to that of the *National Register of Scientific Personnel*. It would eliminate those who perform economic analysis or research but are not professional economists as defined above (accountants, engineers, etc.).

were some 15,000 economists in the United States in 1970.[8] A striking fact is at once obvious; the profession is extremely small. At the same time, for example, there were more than 200,000 physicians and a somewhat larger number of lawyers in the United States. Using a very broad definition, the Census Bureau classified 22,424 persons as economists in the 1960 Census of Occupations, but most professionals would think this figure too high and the definition too loose.

SOME ALTERNATIVE DEFINITIONS

While the definition of an economist which has been cited is the one used in this study, it is obvious that others might be used and that there are numerous persons referring to themselves as economists or holding Civil Service ratings as economists who fail to meet those standards. The most restrictive definition of a professional economist would involve a combination of graduate training and work activity and might read: "Possession of the Ph.D. degree in economics and employment as an economist in business, government, or an academic institution." This definition would clearly eliminate many who are considered or who consider themselves economists. This standard is, except for the academic world, unrealistic at the present time. A more liberal standard might require: "Employment as an economist with more modest educational credentials (i.e., a master's degree in economics, the M.B.A., or some other degree)." The most liberal definition of all ignores formal training and simply requires: "Employment as an economist." This definition would cover large numbers of federal service and business economists whose professional training, if any, is in other fields.

The first definition is the standard most often used by institutions of higher education for recruitment of staff at tenure level. The second definition is more likely to be applied in various higher

[8] There are various alternative definitions—some more liberal, some tighter—but the NSF standard seems reasonable and is widely used. See also Committee on the National Science Foundation Report in the Economics Profession, "The Structure of Economists' Employment and Salaries, 1964," *American Economic Review*, Vol. LV, No. 4, Pt. 2 (December, 1965); National Science Foundation, *Summary of American Science Manpower*, 70–5 (Washington, D.C.: National Science Foundation, 1970); and Nancy Ruggles, ed., *Economics*, Behavioral and Social Sciences Survey (Englewood Cliffs, N.J.: Prentice-Hall, Inc., 1970), especially Chapt. 2.

level Civil Service positions, community college teaching, and business. The third definition is, of course, the most liberal and is based solely on a person's employment as an economist without regard to his training. This definition would be likely to cover run-of-the-mill Civil Service positions and many business activities.

The history of professions, of course, clearly illustrates the trend toward more precise definition of qualifications with increasing emphasis on formal education. Within the present century the practice of medicine has shifted from a mixture of scientific training and apprenticeship to a sharply and legally defined profession. Law and professional engineering have taken the same path in even more recent years.[9] In the future the professional requirements for economists no doubt will be codified with specific educational requirements and will perhaps approximate the most restrictive definition which has been mentioned. The National Science Foundation definition which we have noted is similar to the second definition and is a reasonable standard at the present time except in the academic world. As we shall see in Chapter 3, the academic community considers the Ph.D. a basic career requirement and adds to it such requisites for advancement as research and publication. Clearly, at the present time there are really two basic definitions of the professional economist, one for the academic world and one for the nonacademic world.

The NSF data provide information about the employment of economists as follows:

Type of Employment	Percent Employed
Educational Institutions	44.7
Federal Government	11.3
Other Government	2.5
Industry and Business	34.0
All Other (Military Service, Self-Employed, Other Nonprofit Institutions, etc.)	6.5

[9] Although law and professional engineering are now open only to the professionally trained, large numbers in both professions have had very informal training. As late as the 1940s many states allowed candidates for the bar to "read law," and professional engineering standards are even more recent.

Three main activities—teaching, employment in business, and federal service—account for 91 percent of the total, with academic employment alone claiming almost half.[10]

As will become apparent, there is some overlap in these categories. Some academic economists play dual roles, and to a lesser extent federal and business economists engage in academic pursuits. Only 483 of those economists reporting were women, although that number is probably growing. About fifteen percent of those reporting were between 20 and 29, fifty-nine percent were in the 30 to 40 bracket, and the remainder were 50 or older. Economists generally are highly educated: 41 percent held the Ph.D. degree, 34.6 percent had a master's degree, 21.5 percent possessed a bachelor's degree, some 3 percent had other degrees, and a few had no degree at all.[11] This situation is rapidly changing as more emphasis is placed on advanced degrees.

A rough profile of the economist begins to emerge. His profession is small and not conspicuous to the public eye. His field is dominated by men, most of whom have a great deal of formal education; and all but roughly 10 percent of his colleagues are engaged in one of three major activities. Since so many are employed in higher education, federal service, and large businesses, their geographic distribution is not surprisingly very uneven. The northeastern United States accounts for the greater portion. Except for those in academic life, they are almost never found in small communities.

The National Register of Scientific and Technical Personnel lists, by state of residence, 13,150 persons whose field of competence is economics. Two areas, New York with 1,850 and Washington, D.C. with 1,255, account for 3,105 economists or a bit less than one-fourth of the total. Another 1,215 were in California. Wyoming had only 13, and twenty-two states had fewer than 100. As one would expect, the profession was very unevenly distributed with the three geographic areas noted accounting for the bulk of nonacademic employment.[12] Even among the scientific fields, economics is of modest size. Again let us consult the *Register*.

[10] Committee on the National Science Foundation, "The Structure of Economists' Employment and Salaries," p. 21.

[11] *Ibid.*, p. 19.

[12] For example, in the Washington area there are probably seventy-five to one hundred economists in full-time academic jobs out of the total twelve hundred. In other states (e.g., Nevada with twenty-three) academic employment accounts for almost all. These data are confirmed by the *Directory* of

Among the various fields listed, chemistry was the largest with 65,917, followed by biological sciences and physics with 29,133 and 29,130, respectively. Only agricultural sciences with 10,038 and anthropology with 4,559 were smaller than economics. Not only is the profession small in size, it is also inconspicuous since the economist's work is generally behind the scenes. Most economists in business or government are engaged in research or analysis which seldom makes exciting reading for the layman.

A Note on Black Economists

Economists, like most professionals, are concerned with the status of blacks in the field. As in many other professions, the field has been overwhelmingly dominated by whites. Estimates of the number of black economists range from less than one hundred to several hundred, but it is evident that the number is small.[13]

Many if not most black economists are in academic life or federal service.[14] For many years these economists were concentrated in predominantly black schools, but since the mid-1960s they have found increasing opportunities as students and faculty members at prestige institutions and in the business community. The status of blacks in the field is of particular current interest since there seems to be a well-accepted relationship between economic issues and the problems of blacks.[15]

Great efforts are being made to increase the number of blacks in the field and to improve the number and level of economic course

---

the American Economic Association, which lists place of residence. See *AEA Handbook,* 1969.

[13] See Cleveland A. Chandler, "An Affirmative Action Plan for the Economics Profession," *American Economic Review,* Papers and Proceedings, Eighty-second Annual Meeting, American Economic Association, Vol. LXI, No. 2 (May, 1970), pp. 416ff. For a survey of recent literature dealing with this problem, see Andrew Brimmer and Harriett Harper, "Economists' Perception of Minority Economic Problems: A View of Emerging Literature," *Journal of Economic Literature,* Vol. VIII, No. 3 (September, 1970), pp. 783ff.

[14] Probably the most highly placed black economist is Andrew Brimmer, a member of the Board of Governors of the Federal Reserve System and a former professor at the University of Pennsylvania.

[15] See Gary S. Becker, *The Economics of Discrimination* (Chicago: University of Chicago Press, 1957); and Lester C. Thurow, *Poverty and Discrimination* (Washington, D.C.: Brookings Institution, 1960). By mid-1970 a new journal, *The Review of Black Political Economy* (published by the Black Economic Research Center in New York City) had made its appearance.

offerings at predominantly black schools. These schools historically have tended to stress the humanities, and business or economics courses have often been neglected, as have engineering and the physical sciences.

If one accepts that there are 300 black economists (reportedly, 126 black economists attended the American Economic Association meeting in 1969), and a total of 15,000 professional economists, the black participation rate is only about 2 percent and is quite likely lower. Blacks have made more progress in other professions, but solid figures are hard to find. For example, according to the January, 1970, *Journal* of the American Society of Engineering Education, accredited schools of engineering in the United States granted 35,400 engineering degrees of all types in 1969, of which 139 went to blacks. Law, medicine, and elementary and secondary education have long been among the fields with the largest number of black participants. However, until recent years even these fields generally maintained separate professional associations for blacks, and the degree of real professional integration has been limited.

What Is Economics?

Most people who read this book will have had some acquaintance with economics as an academic subject, but it would be difficult to understand much about economists and their work if one knew nothing at all about economics as a field. Although every elementary textbook includes a brief definition of economics, the fact is that defining the field is no simple task.[16] Determining what limits should be placed on economics as a field, for example, is by no means an easy exercise.

John Stuart Mill noted in the 1840s that the definition of a science has almost invariably not preceded but followed the creation of the science itself. "Like the wall of a city," he noted, "it has usually been erected, not as a receptacle for such edificies as might afterwards spring up, but to circumscribe an aggregate already in existence."[17] The great English economist Alfred Marshall (1842–1924), once commented that while most sciences remain relatively fixed in

---

[16] See, for example, Israel Kirzner, *The Economic Point of View* (New York: D. Van Nostrand Co., 1960), especially Chapt. 1.

[17] *Unsettled Questions in Political Economy* (London: Macmillan Co., Ltd., 1844), p. 120.

scope (at least in his day), economics increases with further study.[18] Many authors who have thought deeply about this matter have concluded that no completely acceptable definition of the field can be formulated. Frank H. Knight has said that "it is impossible to draw a clear-cut boundary around the share or domain of human action to be included in economic science."[19]

For most practical purposes, definitions of economics bear some relationship to economics' concern with the problem of scarcity or the problem of adjusting limited means to unlimited wants. One widely used undergraduate text (Bach, *Economics*, p. 9) states that "economics is the study of how the goods and services we want get produced and how they are distributed among us." Paul Samuelson, after a lengthy discussion, offers a five-part definition which includes exchange, choice, various uses of limited resources, men making a living (producing), and wealth. Most modern economists would not find fault with any of these statements about the subject matter of economics.

Precision of definition generally increases as the subject matter becomes more formalized. Although the definition comes into sharper focus, the depth of the subject matter increases. There is now less overlap between economics and political science or history than was true a century ago, but today's economist has to master a larger and more specific body of knowledge if he is to consider himself an economist. In short, the subject matter is narrower but deeper.

Some Facts on Foreign Economists

While this book is largely concerned with the American economist, it is well to note that economists perform much the same function throughout the world, though of course the political-economic system under which they live makes a great difference in the way they go about their business. Thus while a Soviet economist is, like his American counterpart, concerned with the basic problem of scarcity, his solution to the problem will be found within the general framework of communism instead of capitalism. Despite methodological differences, economists throughout the world share many charac-

---

[18] A. C. Pigou, *Memorials to Alfred Marshall* (London: Macmillan Co., Ltd., 1925), p. 499.

[19] "The Nature of Economic Science in Some Recent Discussion," *American Economic Review*, Vol. XXIV, No. 2 (June, 1934), p. 226.

teristics. Generally, they are broad gauge thinkers (often suspect in totalitarian nations).[20]

Most Western European nations and emerging nations engage in much more economic planning than the United States does, and they utilize economists in large numbers for this purpose. Underdeveloped nations with modest resources must plan very carefully, and much of what is done in the more advanced nations through the market system is done in these nations by the planning mechanism.

Though they may operate under different systems, economists, like other scientists, exchange views and ideas (the Fifth International Congress of Economic History, for example, was held in Leningrad in 1970). Visiting professors, advisers, and others travel; and at any given time, there will be many foreign economists in the United States and American economists in foreign nations.

Few reliable data are available on the number of economists in the world as a whole, their work, and their education. Such evidence as is available indicates that in most parts of the world economists are inclined to devote their talents to government, that they are somewhat less concentrated in academia, and that relatively few are in the business world. The American Economic Association seems to be unique (there are associations of economists in other countries but none so comprehensive) and includes foreign members from ninety-six nations. These data, though fragmentary, are of interest. The communist nations are not well represented. In 1969 a single member was listed from the USSR and two from Yugoslavia. Only a handful represented the more recently created African nations (one from the Ivory Coast and two from Zambia, for example). The AEA lists more than 2,000 members in Western Europe, 477 in Latin America, and more than 1,000 in Asia.

Large numbers of these economists have probably been educated in the United States, Great Britain, or Western Europe. Economics has always been a strong academic area in German and British universities, and it is likely that many economists, especially those in areas formerly under British domination, acquired their advanced training in England.

Associations of economists exist in Argentina, Australia and New

[20] See Calvin B. Hoover, *The Economy, Liberty and the State* (New York: Twentieth Century Fund, 1958).

Zealand, Austria, Belgium, Bolivia, Bulgaria, Canada, Cyprus, Czechoslovakia, Denmark, England, Egypt, Finland, France, Germany (both East and West), Ghana, Greece, Hong Kong, Hungary, India, Israel, Italy, Japan, Korea, Malaysia, Mexico, the Netherlands, Norway, Pakistan, the Philippines, Poland, Portugal, Romania, Spain, South Africa, Sweden, Switzerland, Turkey, the USSR, and Yugoslavia. All these groups are to some degree tied together through the International Economic Association and through this group meet periodically on a worldwide basis.

Having said something about the economist and the field, let us now turn to the way in which he works, to his methodology.

2
The Economist, Methodology, and Philosophy

B USINESS and government economists are becoming increasingly influential. Nonetheless, the academic economists, because they are most often writers and most frequently perform basic research, dominate the advanced thinking of the profession. Government and business economists must, with few exceptions, devote their efforts to applied matters, that is to "economic engineering," whereas one hopes that the leaders among academics are turning their hands to problems on the frontiers of the science.[1]

Methodology

Economics is sometimes divided into three categories—descriptive, analytical, and applied. Descriptive economics gathers all available facts about such given topics as the "International Trade Position of the U.S., 1885–1914," or the "Economy of Canada Before 1900." Analytical economics, using available data, attempts to explain economic phenomena by use of economic theory, econometrics, or the construction of economic models. Applied economics strives to use economic description and theory to explain or predict various eco-

---

[1] Some large physical science firms engage in a degree of pure research as well as applied (Bell Laboratories, for example). Pure research may have only long-range results, but the firm which can afford it may find it worthwhile. There is no evidence that business economists perform pure research at company expense. In fact, relatively few universities perform organized pure economic research, although much is done by individuals or through private or foundation funding. Bureaus of economic research funded by university (state) funds prefer to concentrate on applied problems which please the legislature and the business community.

nomic events. Business and government economists deal largely with applied economics while academic economists deal more often with the descriptive and analytical approaches. All three categories can be subdivided into microeconomics and macroeconomics.

Economic analysis, like economics itself, is often associated with the "scarcity problem," with unlimited wants that cannot all be satisfied because resources are limited. "Micro" and "macro" imply, of course, small and large or individual and aggregate. Therefore, analysis of scarcity problems faced by individuals or firms, such as how a firm can operate efficiently given its internal and external situation, are generally considered to be "microeconomics."[2] Microeconomics is concerned with the small unit—the firm, the market, or the individual. Many "micro" problems are closely related to business management and are akin to fields (at least in practice) such as operations research. "Macroeconomics," on the other hand, consists of analysis of scarcity problems faced by society or the nation as a whole and relates to such issues as how government can satisfy defense and nondefense needs, given anticipated tax receipts and prevailing attitudes toward changes in the public debt.[3]

One textbook distinguishes between micro- and macroeconomics as follows:

On the theoretical level, it is again true that what is valid in a specific instance may not be true of the sum total. If we could simply analyze the operation of a single firm and assume that the economy as a whole is really only one big firm, there would be no need to study macroeconomics or to develop theories of macroeconomic behavior. But macroeconomics is set apart as a separate discipline with its own rules because aggregate economic behavior does not correspond to the summation of individual activities. We may, for example, find that if wages, and therefore production costs, fall, a single firm will find it profitable to expand out-

[2] For texts which deal with such problems, see Joel Dean, *Managerial Economics* (Englewood Cliffs, N.J.: Prentice-Hall, Inc., 1951); Milton H. Spencer and Louis Siegelman, *Managerial Economics* (Homewood, Ill.: Richard D. Irwin, 1959); Leonard W. Weiss, *Case Studies in American Industry* (New York: Wiley & Sons, Inc., 1967); Vivian Charles Walsh, *Introduction to Contemporary Microeconomics* (New York: McGraw-Hill Book Co., 1970); and W. David Maxwell, *Price Theory and Applications in Business Administration* (Pacific Palisades: Goodyear Publishing Co., 1970).

[3] See, for example, Chapt. 3 of *The Economic Report of the President* (Washington, D.C.: Government Printing Office, February, 1970).

put and therefore hire more workers. For the economy as a whole it does not follow that a wage cut will lead to a general expansion of employment. Similarly, one individual, in borrowing from another, borrows a claim over real resources which he must pay back at some future date by giving up a claim over real resources. The community as a whole cannot borrow real resources from itself in one year and pay these resources back in another year. Yet despite this obvious truth the fiction persists that World War II remains to be paid for and that the economic product of future generations is mortgaged to the follies of the past. Similarly, if one individual plans to increase his saving by consuming less, he will, given the necessary self-control, be successful. But if the community as a whole makes such an effort, the reduction in total consumption expenditures may lead to such a shrinkage in income that aggregate saving may be less than before.[4]

Macroeconomics is very broad indeed and encompasses most problems of public policy. Two forces, the Great Depression of the 1930s and the Second World War, had a major influence on macroeconomic development. The former, which focused worldwide attention on problems of employment and national income (much stimulated by Lord Keynes's landmark book, *The General Theory of Employment Interest and Money,* published in 1936), culminated in the United States with the Employment Act of 1946. This act brought in its train tremendous problems of allocation and made essential much greater knowledge of the aggregate economy.[5]

[4] From *Macroeconomics* by Thomas F. Dernburg and Duncan M. McDougall, pp. 2–3. Copyright 1960 by McGraw-Hill Book Company. Used with permission of McGraw-Hill Book Company.

[5] The "Keynesian Revolution" is treated in such works as Robert Lekachman, *The Age of Keynes* (New York: Random House, Vintage Books, 1968); Daniel Fusfeld, *The Age of the Economist* (Glenview: Scott Foresman & Co., 1966); Seymour Harris, *The New Economics* (New York: Alfred A. Knopf, Inc., 1957); and Dudley Dillard, *The Economics of John Maynard Keynes* (Englewood Cliffs, N.J.: Prentice-Hall, Inc., 1946).

For the development and analysis of national income, see Dernburg and McDougall, *Macroeconomics;* Thomas C. Schelling, *National Income Behavior* (New York: McGraw-Hill Book Co., 1951); Paul Samuelson, *Economics* (New York: McGraw-Hill Book Co., 1971); George Bach, *Economics* (Englewood Cliffs, N.J.: Prentice-Hall, Inc., 1966); Charles L. Schultze, *National Income Analysis* (Englewood Cliffs, N.J.: Prentice-Hall, Inc., 1964); Arthur M. Okun, *The Battle Against Unemployment* (New York: W. W. Norton & Co., 1965), and *The Political Economy of Prosperity* (Washington, D.C.: Brookings Institution, 1971); Walter W. Heller, *New Dimensions in Political Economy* (Cambridge, Mass.: Harvard University Press, 1966); and E. Ray Canterbery, *Economics on a New Frontier* (Belmont: Wadsworth Publishing Co., 1968).

Another economic approach centers less on theory and more on observation of data. Empirical economics, which many government and business economists would use in their work, is based on the collection and analysis of economic data observed over a period of time. A purely empirical approach to economics is similar to the method of analysis generally employed by physical scientists. The inputs of the analysis must be facts, hypotheses, or assumptions which can be refuted or confirmed. If assumptions are used, the economist must defend their reasonableness, although he has some leeway. The logical deductions obtained from these assumptions may be elegant and intuitively appealing, but the process is not "science" until the assumptions are shown to be true. The results of the analysis, which are often expressed as predictions, must also be verifiable.

Academic economists have never done a great deal of purely empirical work. In some cases, especially when the required observations are market information (such as trends in the daily volume of sales on the New York Stock Exchange or in annual sales of new automobiles), the data already exist and only need to be put together in some orderly fashion.[6]

In other cases (rates of unemployment or inflation, for instance), the required data are not automatically generated by normal, everyday economic activity and often must be estimated on the basis of available information. War, depression, and the resulting great extension of policy have greatly increased the amount of data available.

Technology and Methodology

Traditionally, economics attracted those who were searching for solutions to problems, and methodology was secondary. Today, however, one often has the impression that many economists are much more interested in the solution than the problem and that the aggregate subject matter is of little importance. Many theoretical economists might be equally interested in radio astronomy or solid-state physics, as long as an esoteric approach is required.

Earlier generations were attracted to the real problems of life. The classical economists were largely problem oriented, as were the

---

[6] Economics, like other sciences, has of course benefited from the development of the computer, which has made great masses of data useful since they can be subjected to processes such as multiple correlation. Aggregate economic data on the national level would have been impossible to analyze by hand.

early American writers. One would hope that the man of powerful intellect is attracted by both the problems and the apparatus used to solve them. Alfred Marshall, the English economist referred to in Chapter 1, was apparently such a person.

Marshall, like many economists with superior intellectual equipment, went through several periods of interest in diverse fields before he became engaged with political economy. Keynes quotes Marshall's progression and his developing social awareness as follows:

> From Metaphysics I went to Ethics, and thought that the justification of the existing condition of society is not easy. A friend, who had read a great deal of what are now called the Moral Sciences, constantly said: "Ah! if you understood Political Economy you would not say that." So I read Mill's *Political Economy* and got much excited about it. I had doubts as to the propriety of inequalities of *opportunity*, rather than of material comfort. Then, in my vacations I visited the poorest quarters of several cities and walked through one street after another, looking at the faces of the poorest people. Next, I resolved to make as thorough a study as I could of Political Economy.[7]

Marshall's mode of entry into the field was typical of his generation as well as of most American economists in the early years of economics.[8]

Of the mature American economists now working, most were attracted to the field by their observations of the Great Depression of the mid-1930s. The manner in which outstanding economists became engaged in the field is of great interest and warrants further study.[9] Questions next come to mind about the future if the affluence of society continues and the range of serious economic problems narrows. Affluence has, of course, had an effect and has changed the problems. Today's economists can concern themselves with the economics of pollution, whereas economists in 1935 would have been delighted to see smoke pouring from factory stacks.

[7] *Essays in Biography* (London: Macmillan Co. Ltd., 1933), pp. 165–66.

[8] Keynes also notes in *Essays in Biography* that F. Y. Edgeworth, another famous English economist, was uninterested in social purpose and only cared about the "science" of economics. Keynes personally was more like Marshall.

[9] See, for example, Joseph A. Schumpeter, *Ten Great Economists* (New York: Oxford University Press, 1951). See also Paul Samuelson, "Economists and the History of Ideas" (presidential address to the AEA), *American Economic Review*, Vol. LII, No. 1 (March, 1962).

Beginning about 1950, great changes began in the technique and teaching of economics. Before that time the work was often "institutional." Specifically, much time was devoted to description of how economic institutions worked while little time was devoted to the aggregate, analytical aspects of the field. Textbooks in use before the 1950s reflected this approach. Few undergraduates majoring in economics had much background in mathematics, and among professionals only those interested in microtheory made use of it. However, the change was very rapid in the 1950s and 1960s. On the undergraduate level this change was symbolized by the publication in 1948 of Paul Samuelson's *Economics*. By 1971 this book was in its eighth edition and in wide use as an introductory textbook.[10]

On every level, economics has become highly quantitative. Mathematics and statistics have invaded the graduate level in a fashion unforeseen twenty years ago, and this has many advantages. Mathematics has given the economist a tool of great usefulness and has vastly increased the precision and range of analysis.

National income analysis, for example, which had been considered quite sophisticated in 1945, began to be taught routinely in introductory courses. By 1965 most large departments were incorporating simple computer "games" involving national income concepts into the sophomore course, an unheard-of idea two decades earlier. There are also serious problems attending the increased emphasis on mathematics. No doubt students who might in the ordinary course of events have some interest in a career in economics shy away because they doubt their mathematical skills. In addition, the professional reliance on mathematics has made it more difficult for the economist to communicate with his lay audience. This situation is unfortunate since the economist's increasing authority is thus often lost on the layman.

Much current economic analysis, especially on the national scene, requires vast amounts of data which were not available three decades ago. One contribution made by pioneer government economists was the establishment of machinery to gather and compile, on a systematic basis, data about the aggregate economy. These data can also be

[10] Samuelson, a professor of economics at MIT and a frequent adviser to federal officials (he was a favorite of JFK), is one of the most influential economists now living and received the Nobel Prize in 1970.

used by theorists to give reality to and to check the validity of their models and simulations.

While an empirical economist may be gathering data and drawing conclusions about the economy of Appalachia, his theory-oriented colleague may be constructing an elaborate model (perhaps involving hundreds of complex equations) of a part of the economy. Recent issues of the *American Economic Review*, for example, contain the following articles which illustrate the theoretical approach to real economic issues: "The Cost of the Draft and the Cost of Ending the Draft" (Fisher), "Behavior of the Firm under Regulatory Constraint" (Takayama), "An Econometric Model of Development" (Adelman and Morris), and "International Productivity Differences" (Melvin). As might be expected, a wide variety of work utilizing various methods of investigation is carried on by academic, government, and business economists, depending upon the nature of the problem.[11]

One difficulty which faces economists, as well as other scientists, is the fact that the frontiers of knowledge advance rapidly. What was a decade ago the subject of research by outstanding men in the field is today incorporated into the general body of knowledge— "textbook stuff." Kelvin Lancaster, speaking of mathematical economics, notes that its scope is changing constantly since "it acts as a port of entry for new analytical techniques. . . . Yesterday's advanced mathematical economics is today's mathematical economics, and will be tomorrow's economic analysis."[12]

Pioneering work in attacking the more esoteric problems has for the most part been done by the academic theorist, although one must also give some credit to the government economist (often a former academician), who has been in the forefront of such matters as national income accounting and forecasting.

Specialists Versus Generalists

The growth of professionalism brought another development common to most fields, the rise of the specialist. Most early economists

---

[11] See, for example, Robert Ferber and P. J. Verdoorn, *Research Methods in Economics and Business* (New York: Macmillan Co., 1962); and J. Francis Rummel and Wesley C. Ballaine, *Research Methods in Business* (New York: Harper and Row, 1963).

[12] *Mathematical Economics* (New York: Macmillan Co., 1968), p. 1.

were, as we have seen, generalists in every sense of the word. Theologians, philosophers, lawyers, and engineers who dabbled in political economy, they were, like David Hume, patron saints of half a dozen modern sciences. Today's economist is apt to be a monetary economist, an international economist, or some other special variety of economist. Those who remain generalists are most often in the academic world and tend to emphasize undergraduate teaching. As in law and medicine, prestige and financial reward have gone to those who "learn more and more about less and less." One would, of course, expect to find this tendency among government and business economists, especially those at intermediate levels since they must work on circumscribed problems. Specialization is, after all, a function of job content. However, the trend is equally strong among academics.

Increased specialization has, to be sure, made the economist more useful in government and business, and this trend is likely to continue in all areas. However, one problem is the sheer bulk of material facing the generalist. In all, the well-rounded and well-read general economist would be required to read some twenty or thirty journals in the United States alone, plus many foreign journals. Even abstracts of major articles covered more than one hundred pages in a recent issue of the *Journal of Economic Literature,* and reviews of new books occupied sixty pages. In both cases only a sampling was provided, for many books are never reviewed, and many other journals also carry reviews.[13] Clearly, the specialist does well if he reads at least one general journal in addition to the two or three journals in his area of specialization. The generalist who hopes to keep up with the entire field of economics faces a gigantic task.

Specialization naturally has tended to fragment the field. Not only is the specialist saying more and more about less, but he is also apt to isolate himself from his fellows. The proliferation of journals is a portent of this trend. Repelled at least in part by the theory and mathematical orientation of the *American Economic Review,* and with growing literature in their own special fields, economists have

[13] There are dozens more when one considers periodicals and occasional papers published by academic bureaus of economic research, Federal Reserve banks, the International Monetary Fund, the U.S. Department of Agriculture, etc.

splintered off and begun such journals as *Business Economics,* the *Anti-Trust Law and Economics Review,* and the *Journal of Economic Education.*[14]

As we have seen, early economists in the United States and abroad, especially the laymen, were generally concerned with practical issues in which theory was merely a tool. Academic economists, on the other hand, concentrated on "science" and tended to separate themselves not only from their lay associates but also from their more pragmatic professional colleagues.

Allan Gruchy has characterized the "scientific attitude of the academic economist in the early years of the century" as follows:

> By 1900 academic American economics was back in the same intellectual groove in which it had been in 1800; that is to say, it was once more under the influence of the mechanistic intellectual orientation which had been so popular at the beginning of the nineteenth century. Although a considerable refinement of the main body of orthodox economic thought had been achieved in the century after 1800, the spirit and essence of the science as it was taught in most university class rooms remained substantially unaltered all during the century.[15]

In contrast to academic economists' theory orientation, those who were first accepted into both government and business had a practical and applied outlook. The "political economists" of the New Deal years were, with some exceptions, not adherents to the view that economics was a pure science. Those who came after the Second World War and those who have become influential in business have demonstrated considerable technical expertise, but they are understandably concerned with applied problems. These economists tend to combine a mastery of technique with a desire to apply their ability as analysts.

The Power Structure

Theodore White, journalist and observer of the American scene, has spoken of an intellectual establishment or "priesthood" consisting

---

[14] In 1971 some twenty-five journals written in English were devoted to economics per se, and more than twenty others were devoted to such fringe areas as accounting, marketing, and management.

[15] Allan G. Gruchy, *Modern Economic Thought* (Englewood Cliffs, N.J.: Prentice-Hall, Inc., 1947), pp. 12–13.

of various academic persons who are, for the most part, in residence at prestige universities in the Northeast. These "power brokers," including academic economists, are active in politics and vendors of ideas, and they have become a significant political force. White has suggested that the "back room politician" has been somewhat displaced, at least on the national scene, by the "back room scholar."[16] It has been suggested that this "priesthood" would be difficult for the nonestablishment economist to penetrate, and to some degree this may be true.

Joseph Spengler believes that a monopoly of opinion is less likely now than formerly because many fads and trends come and go and are always fighting for attention.[17] However, both Spengler and Martin Bronfenbrenner, after considering this matter at length, do see some danger that creators of thought will develop a consensus which will later ossify into an orthodoxy that retards progress.[18] The enormous variety of literature and the growing multiplicity of journals nonetheless seem to indicate that everyone will have a chance to have his say. Likewise, the number of publishers accepting books on economics has greatly increased, with the result that a good manuscript, even though unorthodox, is likely to find an outlet. Of course, one must admit that the prestige of journals varies widely, and it does make a difference where an author has his say. An article in one of the top journals would be much more influential than the identical article published in a more pedestrian organ. Similarly, a prestige university press is a better vehicle for a book than an unknown publisher.

There is little doubt, however, that a number of academic economists have a mental map of the United States which, except for small islands, does not include the vast area between the Hudson River and the eastern border of California or the region south of the Potomac.

Members of the Council of Economic Advisers, informal advisers to presidential candidates, and other economists who play national

[16] See Joseph J. Spengler, "Economics: Its History, Themes, and Approaches," *Journal of Economic Issues*, Vol. 12 (March, 1968), p. 20.

[17] See also G. William Donhoff, *The Higher Circles* (New York: Random House, Inc., 1970), especially Chapt. 6. Copyright Random House, Inc.

[18] Martin Bronfenbrenner, "Trends, Cycles, and Fads in Economic Writing," *American Economic Review*, Vol. LV, No. 2 (May, 1966), pp. 529ff.

roles have come from a relatively small list of schools and generally espouse orthodox ideas. This list includes, in the East, Columbia, Harvard, MIT, and Yale; in the Midwest, Chicago, Michigan, and Minnesota; and in the Far West, Stanford and the University of California at Berkeley. Harvard, Columbia, and Yale combined, for example, provided nine of the twenty-three CEA members who had served by 1968. Walter Heller was from the outpost of Minnesota and John P. Lewis from Indiana. Many early high-level advisers in government were from the Brookings Institution.[19]

Many scholars cite the American Association of Graduate Schools as a powerful and somewhat exclusive group with great prestige on the national level, especially in research activity. While not all of the forty-two schools belonging to this group in 1970 are strong in economics, they are, in general, top drawer institutions. Only one, Colorado, is in the Rocky Mountain area; and in the South, Duke, Vanderbilt, Virginia, Texas, North Carolina at Chapel Hill, and Tulane are the sole representatives.

Economists in these institutions are often in the forefront of research, publish widely, advise government officials, and recommend others to serve as advisers. Their more academic colleagues publish pioneering work (often heavily funded by grants), edit the scholarly journals, and are generally in what is widely considered the vanguard of the profession. Virtually by definition, great work is done by renowned scholars in prestige schools. Just how one breaks into the circle is hard to say. Money, past reputation, and other factors are all important.[20] Also, the academic economist belongs to a small group in which personal contacts are important. A promising young man in a prestige institution therefore will find doors opened to him by his seniors which unfortunately will remain firmly locked to an equally qualified man from an obscure institution. The "stock

---

[19] Brookings, a Washington research institution, specializes in economics and the social sciences. Edwin G. Nourse, the first CEA chairman, and other federal economists have been or are associated with it. Between 1924 and 1928, Brookings offered the Ph.D. but abandoned the program. Kermit Gordon, its president, is an economist and formerly was federal budget director in the Kennedy-Johnson years. See Charles B. Saunders, *The Brookings Institution: A Fifty Year History* (Washington, D.C.: Brookings Institution, 1966).

[20] For example, a small and impoverished school often cannot attract enough well-qualified men to become accredited: well-qualified men cannot afford to go to an unaccredited institution.

exchange" of academic reputation changes slowly; a reputation as a strong school is hard to gain, and hard to lose.

Young Turks on the March

As in most professions in this era of rapid change, one sees among economists, especially the young, a tendency to ignore established lines and to question hitherto accepted practices. A young economist has characterized his generation as follows:

Almost by definition, the new scientists are young. Youth is more than a matter of chronological age with them, it is a quality of spirit— they have the wings of the morning. If we must have a name for these scientific revolutionaries, I shall adopt one that is going around and call them the "Young Turks."

I cannot give a list of characteristics that any Young Turk would necessarily possess; but I can sketch some typical qualities. They tend to be mathematicians, which accounts for part of their elegance and style—and indeed for their artistic streak, since it is well known that mathematicians always were noted for this characteristic. They are mathematicians of the new kind, preoccupied with issues of form, which are largely involved with logical structure and are in a sense sometimes philosophical.

They are devastatingly successful but they do not worship the bitch goddess success. Of course, they do not need to. They are the first generation of American academics not acquainted in their own lives with problems about money. A Young Turk may drive a Ferrari or a Volkswagen but he will choose his car because it suits him and not because he needs to keep up with the Joneses (or even with the Armstrong-Joneses). And he is likely to be dressed in a way that makes cops hostile, unless he is dressed very well indeed by a Carnaby Street tailor —and that could make cops hostile too.[21]

Though no doubt overdrawn and a bit arrogant in tone, this characterization contains grains of truth worth contemplating.

In both 1968 and 1969 dissident groups of young economists made their views known at the annual meeting of the American Economic Association. However, unlike the Modern Language Association,

[21] From *Introduction to Contemporary Micro-economics* by Vivian C. Walsh, p. 4. Copyright 1970 by McGraw-Hill Book Company. Used with permission of McGraw-Hill Book Company.

where a take-over was performed at the business meeting, those who protested at the AEA meeting were vocal but orderly.

The Radical Movement

The radical economists are following a well-accepted tradition to a surprising degree, for radicals have always been an active element in the profession. Given the conventional wisdom of their eras, such economists as Thorstein Veblen and Richard T. Ely were "radical" indeed.

What are the goals of the current "radical" economists, and how do they differ from those of the "conventional" economists? Many current radicals do not accept the concept of capitalism held by most of their conventional associates. For example, many radicals claim that the war in Vietnam was an imperialistic exercise and that conventional economics' only comment on the war is about how to finance it efficiently. These economists are concerned with what they see as the consequences of capitalism, including income inequality, destruction of the environment, racism, oppression of women, and alienation between classes in society. Radicals, and many who would reject the term as describing themselves, feel that the "Samuelson-Solow generation" (although not necessarily Samuelson and Solow themselves), was apt to pay too much attention to methodology and not enough to the social and human relations aspects of economics.

It is interesting that the radical creed rejects the marginal analysis technique. A few radical economists argue that there is no point in such an exercise because capitalism is not worthy of analysis and that discrete changes make marginal considerations meaningless.[22] The radicals often strongly object to economists who lend their talents to the Defense Department, CIA, or organizations such as the Institute for Defense Analysis. Nonradical economists probably would not object to this type of service as long as it was, in their view, technically interesting and professionally rewarding.

Many "radical" or "liberal" economists accept capitalism as a basic framework but raise serious questions about some of its institutions and effects, just as Veblen and Ely did in their era and John Kenneth Galbraith did in the 1960s. Many radicals conclude that such broad social goals as housing, clean air, education, and

---

[22] See, for example, Michael Zweig, *A New Left Critique of Radical Economics* (Ann Arbor: Union for Radical Political Economics, 1969).

employment of minority groups are incompatible with the goals of conventional capitalism. The solution to these problems is apt to be noneconomic in nature and thus cannot square with the profit motive.[23] Radicals and indeed many nonradicals argue that capitalism has been so engrossed in the pursuit of economic growth that its costs to society have been ignored and that conventional economics has no answer for matters such as black-white relations.[24] Thus the radicals have diverse views and accept or reject conventional economics in varying degrees.

The radical economists' "establishment" is the Union for Radical Political Economics, established in 1968 and headquartered in Cambridge, Massachusetts. The organization publishes the *Review of Radical Political Economics* and, as of 1970, had some six hundred members.[25] This movement is young, and it is hard to say how far or in what direction it will progress. To date radical political economists seem to have made advances mainly in the Ivy League schools and on the West Coast.[26]

Economic assumptions usually have embodied the values of Western society. Insofar as the young constitute the society of the coming decades, their evolving value system will no doubt restructure some common economic constraints. It appears less and less radical when attacks are made on such ideas as economic growth is good at any cost, profits should be maximized without concern for ecological survival, and poverty is a problem for social workers.

Schools of Thought

Economists, especially those in academic life, have often been criticized on the grounds that they are prone to disagree about

[23] See Michael Harrington, *The Accidental Century* (New York: Macmillan Co., 1965).

[24] A good statement of views appears in Richard C. Edwards *et al.*, "A Radical Approach to Economics: Basis for a New Curriculum," *American Economic Review*, Papers and Proceedings, Eighty-second Annual Meeting, American Economic Association, Vol. LXI, No. 2 (May, 1970), pp. 352ff. This curriculum, proposed for Social Sciences 125 in the General Education program at Harvard, is oriented toward such topics as imperialism, destruction of the environment, and subjugation of women.

[25] For a good description of the URPE and its aims see James H. Weaver, "Toward a Radical Political Economics," *The American Economist*, Vol. XIV, No. 1 (Spring, 1970).

[26] See Martin Bronfenbrenner, "Radical Economics in America," *Journal of Economic Literature*, Vol. VIII, No. 3 (September, 1970).

methodology or philosophy and certainly about remedies for various economic ailments. It is likely that these philosophical differences are less pronounced now than formerly and also that the differences are often overstated by noneconomists.

C. E. Ayres notes that among physical scientists differences are continuous but involve detail, whereas among economists differences are more basic.[27] Differences that do exist among physical scientists often pass unseen by the layman since they fail to impress him. Earth scientists, for example, disagree about the origin of the earth, but this matter is of little importance to the average citizen. On the contrary, disagreements among economists about a tax or a tariff will have considerable impact on the layman.

Economists are, like most people, not entirely happy to be classified or labeled according to their philosophies; yet for purposes of discussion it is often necessary to do so. One would hope that the economist, as a scientist, might be capable of performing analysis or rendering economic judgment apart from his personal economic or social preferences. For instance, an economist who personally endorsed socialism and worked toward that end as a citizen should be able as an economist to study, understand, and teach or write about the capitalist system without bias. Obviously, some can and some cannot. Few people would question that a physician would be either more or less capable of removing a brain tumor if he was a communist or a capitalist, for his technical skill as a surgeon would exist apart from his socioeconomic ideas. However, many people, including a large number of economists, would question the ability of a social scientist to act in the same detached manner.

Let us assume that most economists can, or at least try, to compartmentalize their personal and professional philosophies. This dichotomization is probably most true of those whose major interest is in theory. The theoretician generally tries and usually succeeds in adopting the scientific method, within the limitations imposed on him by his cultural background and personal experiences which may "value load" his basic premises in a way in which he cannot even be aware.

Those economists who adopt a professional political philosophy and openly espouse it in writing, speaking, or by entering the public

---

[27] *The Industrial Economy* (Boston: Houghton Mifflin Co., 1952), pp. 1–2.

forum can, of course, be classified. More specifically, those economists who espouse a given line of thought professionally through their employment by trade associations, their active participation in public life, or their efforts to shape public opinion presumably are in sympathy with the goals of the organization. One can hardly imagine an economist who has strong leanings toward the left working for (or being hired by) the U.S. Chamber of Commerce or a strong conservative serving as chairman of the Americans for Democratic Action. However, such a person might very well function in a business firm or government agency if he were doing a technical job as economist rather than serving as propagandist or advocate.

Many academic economists have no hesitation about casting themselves as liberal, conservative, or whatever, and their writings can be so classified. John Kenneth Galbraith has served, for example, as the chairman of the Americans for Democratic Action, a liberal group.[28] Arthur F. Burns, chairman of the Federal Reserve Board of Governors in the Nixon administration, and chairman of the Council of Economic Advisers under Eisenhower, is, by his statement, an economist who happens to be a Republican (some said he was a Republican who happened to be an economist). Generally, few economists take active party roles and seem to prefer to remain independent in a political sense.

In a professional sense, however, they often adhere to a school of thought or, probably in most cases, accept or reject various elements which make up the body of concepts by which the school is identified. Many economists would, for example, reject a simple and clear-cut tag such as liberal, or conservative, claiming that the category was too limited to describe their overall philosophies.

REFORM LIBERALS

The intellectual heirs of the institutional economists are found among the reform liberals. The economists see the development of natural resources, enactment of minimum wage legislation, coordination of transportation, and other concerns as examples of necessary and sound economic policy. Reform liberals distrust, or are at least skeptical of, the mechanism of the market in its uninhibited form,

[28] Galbraith, a Harvard economist and prolific writer, is perhaps the best-known economist in the U.S. to the layman. He was Kennedy's ambassador to India and in 1971 was president of the American Economic Association.

and they place a high value on economic stability and full employment.[29] Perhaps the best and certainly the most popular recent exposition of the reform liberal viewpoint has been given by John Kenneth Galbraith. These economists probably reached their peak of policy influence between 1930 and 1940 when popular discontent with the economic system ran high.[30] The economists who came to maturity during these years of depression were naturally influenced in their thinking by serious cyclical problems which were so apparent during that decade.[31] Gruchy's *Modern Economic Thought* contains a sympathetic account of the ideas held by many influential economists during these years.[32]

Generally speaking, the liberals favor an active governmental role and employ fiscal and monetary policy as well as direct economic controls (wage-price) to achieve desirable economic ends. Economic aid to underprivileged groups, control of monopoly, and quasi-public enterprises are encouraged as means of achieving their major goal, economic stability. Big business is suspect while labor union activity is welcomed.

While liberals consider extensive economic planning desirable, they often give inadequate attention to the long-range goals of the economic system. Where neo-liberals tend to oversimplify, liberals frequently seem to be overly complex, mixing social and economic

---

[29] See John Kenneth Galbraith, *Economics and the Art of Controversy* (New Brunswick: Rutgers University Press, 1955), especially Chapt. 5; *The Affluent Society* (Boston: Houghton Mifflin Co., 1958); and *The New Industrial State* (Boston: Houghton Mifflin Co., 1967). See also Allen M. Sievers, *Revolution and the Economic Order* (Englewood Cliffs, N.J.: Prentice-Hall, Inc., 1962), Chapts. 1 and 2.

The writings of Alvin Hansen illustrate quite clearly the emphasis placed upon stability by these economists. A leading American exponent of the views of Lord Keynes, Hansen has long been an advocate of positive planning and control. See his *Business Cycles and National Income* (New York: W. W. Norton & Co., 1964); *Economic Issues of the 1960's* (New York: McGraw-Hill Book Co., 1960); and *The American Economy* (New York: McGraw-Hill Book Co., 1957).

[30] For a popular account, see Broadus Mitchell, *Depression Decade* (New York: Holt, Rinehart and Winston, 1961).

[31] For example, see Charles J. Hitch, *The Uses of Economics* (Santa Monica: Rand Corporation, 1960), p. 1.

[32] See Chapters 6 through 8. See also Seymour E. Harris, ed., *Saving America's Capitalism: A Liberal Economic Program* (New York: Alfred A. Knopf, Inc., 1948): Alvin Hansen, *Economic Policy and Full Employment* (New York: McGraw-Hill Book Co., 1947); and Gerhard Colm, *Essays in Public Finance and Fiscal Policy* (New York: Oxford University Press, 1955).

matters indiscriminately. Liberals also are apt to put excessive dependence on legislation and regulation as solutions to economic problems. Consequently, many of the more active economic advisers have come from the liberal ranks.

CONSERVATIVES

In general, conservatives view active governmental economic policy with alarm. Monetary policy is acceptable to them, but they believe fiscal policy should be applied with great caution. They also accept control over monopoly and public utilities but feel that aid to businesses or individuals should come from private enterprise insofar as possible. While economic planning is suspect, conservatives put considerable stress on competition, with an appropriate lack of government intervention.[33] More extreme members of this group are apt to let their economic views be influenced by their political and social outlooks (for example, a literal interpretation of the Constitution or the "balanced" budget). They also tend to stress such loosely defined concepts and slogans as "sound money," "constitutional government," and on the negative side, "creeping socialism" and "bureaucracy." Most conservative economists shy away from active roles in public policy except in time of war when they can perform technical services.[34]

NEO-LIBERALS (HIGHLY CONSERVATIVE)

Neo-liberal economists generally view both big business and big government with suspicion. In their view, economic development is the province of private enterprise. Stability is important but is only worthwhile when it is achieved within the framework of free enterprise. Labor unions, if they are to be tolerated at all, should be controlled, as should other monopolies. Neo-liberals give their limited support to such social legislation as unemployment compensation and Social Security.[35] However, while the reform liberals put great faith

[33] See Francis X. Sutton *et al.*, *The American Business Creed* (Cambridge, Mass.: Harvard University Press, 1956); Russell Kirk, *The Conservative Mind* (Chicago: Regency Press, 1953); Walter Lippman, *The Good Society* (New York: Grosset and Dunlap, 1934); and Henry W. Spiegel, *Current Economic Problems* (Homewood, Ill., Richard D. Irwin, 1961).

[34] For a definitive work, see Clinton Rossiter, *Conservatism in America* (New York: Alfred A. Knopf, Inc., 1955).

[35] See Oskar Morgenstern, *The Limits of Economics* (London: Wm. Hodge &

in planning and distrust the "automatic" quality of the market, the neo-liberals put great faith in the market mechanism and strongly favor individual freedom.[36]

Neo-liberals' orientation does not lead them into the ranks of economists who hold public office or are active in business. In general, they are limited to academic pursuits or are in opinion-making groups which are often financed by the extreme right wing and are highly critical of governmental institutions. A relatively small group of economists and dissident intellectuals espouse this line of thought, and most have no large popular following. Neo-liberals hold, as an ideal, an economy made up of small units which strongly emphasize the role of the market. Because, in their view, the market operates as an institution to protect and encourage individual freedom, market controls are both unnecessary and undesirable. Most economists would point out that the neo-liberals have failed to grasp the importance of organizations in the modern society. In fact, they seem to hark back to the economy of the mid-nineteenth century as a model. Neo-liberals have a tendency to oversimplify problems in the economic and social systems. From their perspective, neo-liberals naturally do not look with favor on the federal government's growing involvement in the economy.

THE OLD LEFT

We met the new left in the guise of the radical economists, or at least in some elements of this group. The old left cannot be separated entirely from the new, but the old left has for many years constituted a small but lively group of economists. Those subscribing to Marxian economics have, for the most part, been few in number. A fairly small group of academic economists (generally careful scholars) have long been Marxists although not necessarily admirers of

Co., Ltd., 1937); Fritz Machlup, *The Political Economy of Monopoly* (Baltimore: Johns Hopkins University Press, 1964); F. H. Knight, *The Ethics of Competition* (New York: Harper and Row, 1935); Henry C. Simons, *Economic Policy for a Free Society* (Chicago: University of Chicago Press, 1948); David McCord Wright, *Democracy and Progress* (New York: Macmillan Co., 1948); and John Jewkes, *Ordeal by Planning* (New York: Macmillan Co., 1948).

[36] See Frederick A. Hayek, *The Road to Serfdom* (Chicago: University of Chicago Press, 1944); Ludwig von Mises, *Human Action* (New Haven: Yale University Press, 1949); and Milton Friedman, *Capitalism and Freedom* (Chicago: University of Chicago Press, 1962).

communism as practiced in the Soviet Union, Red China, or Cuba; and most often they have no connection with the Communist party. The late Paul Baran and Paul Sweezy are examples of sound Marxian scholars in recent times.[37]

Perhaps the leading socialist writer of current standing is Michael Harrington, author of *The Accidental Century* (1965), to which we have referred, and *Toward a Democratic Left* (1968). Baran's best-known work is *The Political Economy of Growth* (1957), while Sweezy is probably best known for his *Theory of Capitalist Development* (1942). These scholars, like their opposites on the far right, have never had a wide following. Many of their ideas merge into those of the radicals, although they are of course older and more apt to be classic scholars as are their European counterparts.

Recent Changes in Economic Thinking

Major changes have taken place since 1940 in the role of economists and economic thought in the United States. Men with professional economic training have found their way into higher levels of government and business with far greater frequency and have become increasingly influential. While differences of opinion exist among professional economists, controversy is less evident than it was in 1930 or 1940. One now seldom hears of Keynesian and non-Keynesian economists, since Keynes's relevant work largely has been synthesized into the general body of economics. Many current writers were trained during the 1930s and consequently were greatly influenced by the depression years; but the younger writers and policy makers, trained just before or after World War II, have been subjected to a different set of problems. If full employment and stability were the catchwords of economists in the 1930s, economic growth and development have been for those in the 1950s and the 1960s.

Some controversy, essentially political rather than economic, still exists regarding the role of government in economic affairs. Except among the dedicated neo-liberals, argument centers around the details of government's role rather than around whether government should have a role at all. Professional economists have little doubt

---

[37] A brief exposition of their views for undergraduate reading appears in R. Romano and M. Leiman, eds., *Views of Capitalism* (Beverly Hills: Free Press of Glencoe, 1970), Pt. 3.

about the basic appropriateness of such issues as fiscal policy, minimum wages, unemployment insurance, control over labor relations, and issuance of securities, although there is disagreement about how these matters should be handled.

Since the 1930s economic thinking has been influenced by organized groups.[38] The number of such groups has increased in recent years and will doubtless continue to increase as the impact of public policy becomes more visible. Some are fact-finding and educational groups whose reports are designed to acquaint literate citizens with issues in the modern economy; others peddle a specific line of thought and attempt to win adherents. Perhaps preeminent among the former is the National Bureau of Economic Research, organized in 1920 and famous for its work in the area of business fluctuations. Typical of studies it has produced are Simon Kuznets' *Capital in the American Economy* (1961) and *National Wealth in the United States* (1962), and Wesley C. Mitchell's landmark study, *Business Cycles: The Problem and Its Setting* (1927).

A more recently formed group is the Committee for Economic Development. The CED, broadly based in business as well as academic economics, has produced studies such as *Economic Growth in the U.S.—Its Past and Future, Fiscal and Monetary Policy for High Employment,* and *An Adaptive Program for Agriculture.* Yet another group, the National Planning Association, promotes long-range planning, publishes studies on various economic problems, and makes many economic projections. Typical of its work is *Political Economy in American Foreign Policy* (1954).

These groups play an increasingly significant and expanding role. The sociologist William Donhoff has advanced the thesis that these groups, in cooperation with giant enterprises and large "eastern establishment" law firms, supply both talent and high level personnel to the governmental process.[39] More specifically:

The Council on Foreign Relations is by no means the only power elite link between the corporations and the federal government in the issue-area of foreign policy. There are many others, perhaps the most im-

---

[38] How successful these efforts are is hard to say. Most of these groups are designed to influence students and laymen rather than professionals. Their success is probably quite limited, although the purely educational groups are no doubt more effective than organizations on the extreme right or left.

[39] *The Higher Circles.*

portant of which are the Committee for Economic Development, the RAND Corporation and a handful of research institutes affiliated with elite universities. Turning to the first of these, the Committee for Economic Development (CED) is a tax-exempt research organization which is in many ways the counterpart on economic policy of the Council on Foreign Relations. While its concentration on monetary and economic problems makes it more prominent on issues involving the Departments of Treasury and Commerce, it has on several occasions played a major role in shaping foreign policy.

The relationship of the CED to the corporations really does not need to be established for membership is limited to big businessmen and a handful of university presidents. . . .

Perhaps the best known of the power elite's large research organizations is the RAND Corporation, a name which is an acronym for "research and development." It has been credited with many technical innovations and operational suggestions. Started after the war with government research contracts and Ford Foundation money to "think" for the Air Force, it has since expanded its staff and facilities to provide this service for the entire federal government. Its 500-man professional staff is well-paid and well-educated (150 have Ph.D.'s) due to the fact that RAND was purposely set up as a non-governmental agency so that civil service rules and salary scales could be avoided in order to attract the finest talent money could buy.[40]

Donhoff also analyzes the National Bureau of Economic Research, the Brookings Institution, the Twentieth Century Fund, and the National Planning Association. He holds that these groups have become increasingly important in shaping social legislation and that their close ties with the "establishment" assures that the resulting legislation will be generally conservative in tone. This thesis is probably debatable, but the growing influence of these groups seems to be clearly established. Although the purpose for which they were organized—to provide intellectual guidance to the federal process—has been largely taken over by federal agencies, these groups continue to play an important role by providing views that are independent of the formal federal establishment.

Akin to the CED is the Twentieth Century Fund, which has produced such studies as George W. Stocking's *Cartels in Action* (1946); Albert G. Hart's *Defense and the Dollar* (1953); and per-

[40] *Ibid.*, pp. 123–25.

haps best known, J. Frederick Dewhurst's *America's Needs and Resources* (1955).

The Brookings Institution has studied many policy areas and has published many books and monographs, especially in the areas of traditional regulation such as transport. On the whole, such fact-finding and educational groups are staffed by capable professional economists and maintain a generally high level of sophistication in analysis and discussion. Their influence is difficult to measure, but it must be fairly substantial. Despite whatever shortcomings they may have, there is no doubt that they do at least focus attention on matters of public policy and create interest in policy discussion.

The U.S. Chamber of Commerce, the American Enterprise Association, various labor unions, trade associations such as the Association of American Railroads, and many obscure organizations are typical of those attempting to sell a particular viewpoint. It seems very likely that these groups win few adherents other than those who already hold such views.[41]

In recent years academic economists have become more understanding of business problems. Wartime service gave many of these economists insight into the problems of government and a realistic grasp on the practical aspects of public policy, thus reducing the gulf between the academician and the business community. Aside from the many academic economists engaged in business advisory activities, countless seminars, management programs, and conferences bring economists and businessmen together. Such activities have lowered the barriers between those who teach and observe economic action and those who carry it out, and this situation has likely been beneficial to both parties. Much has been done and much still remains to be done to increase the uniformity in approach and usefulness of economic science. One must of course admit that debate and disagreement have value in that they define issues and generate knowledge. However, all schools and techniques have something to contribute, and the problems are sufficiently pressing to require a variety of efforts. No time and effort can be wasted in intramural warfare.

---

[41] Hundreds of small organizations and single individuals grind out pamphlets advocating free silver, abolition of the income tax, etc. Except in rare instances the writers are not trained economists, their financial base is insecure, and their influence is nil.

3

The Economist
in Academia

THE young professional economist who enters academic life joins the largest group of his colleagues, for in 1970 almost half of all professional economists were still found in college teaching. However, economics came into the academic world at a relatively late date.[1]

Before 1870 economics was rarely found in American institutions of higher learning and indeed faced a struggle for survival. Economics courses, where offered, were seldom independent and most often were appended to such fields as political science or moral philosophy.[2] In fact, at most institutions the term "political economy" was used in place of "economics" until 1900.[3] By the mid-1880s the pace had quickened, and a great deal of interest in the subject had begun to develop as the turn of the century approached. Several reasons can be noted for economics' growing popularity.

For one, the period brought a wide range of new "problems." The nation became increasingly concerned over the value of money, bank

[1] For an interesting account of economics' rise in the academic world, see John B. Parrish, "Rise of Economics as an Academic Discipline: The Formative Years," *Southern Economic Journal*, Vol. XXXIV, No. 1 (July, 1967), pp. 2–16. See also Laurence E. Leamer, "A Brief History of Economics in General Education," *American Economic Review*, The Teaching of Undergraduate Economics, Vol. XL, No. 5 (December, 1950).

[2] See B. F. Kiker and Robert J. Carlsson, eds., *South Carolina Economists: Essays on the Evolution of Antebellum Thought*, Essays in Economics Series, Vol. 20 (Columbia: University of South Carolina Bureau of Business and Economic Research, 1969).

[3] See Joseph Dorfman, "The Department of Economics," in *A History of the Faculty of Political Science* (New York: Columbia University Press, 1955).

failures, agricultural prices and land policy, urban unemployment, taxes, corporate trusts and monopoly, and railroad regulation.[4]

Many complex matters with regard to the growing influence of big business were coming into view, and there was little in the way of an academic framework within which to treat these issues. It would, however, be a mistake to think that academic economists rushed forward with solutions to these problems. Probably the most useful work done by these economists concerned regulating industries in the public utility category, especially the railroads. The regulation of industry (essentially the simulation of competition) seemed well suited to academic economics, but even here the core issues were, or appeared to be, legal rather than economic.

Finding little advanced subject matter at home, many young scholars who hoped for a career teaching economics studied abroad, most often in Germany where economics was not only more highly developed but graduate study in general was more advanced.[5] By 1900 the field had grown, and systematic undergraduate work in economics had become more widely available in the United States. Economic problems abounded, and young economists who earlier had faced a paucity of academic jobs now were in demand.[6]

Although economics as an academic subject had begun to overtake the classics in the 1890s, men who chose the field often had "hard sledding." Economists frequently were caught in cross fire between free traders and protectionists and became involved in other concrete economic issues, to the distress of university presidents and often the wrath of trustees. Nonetheless, by 1900 there were fifty-one chairs in economics and/or political economy in American universities.[7]

---

[4] Parrish, "Rise of Economics as an Academic Discipline," p. 8. See also A. W. Coats, "The American Political Economy Club," *American Economic Review*, Vol. LI (September, 1961); and S. D. Gordon, "Attitudes Toward Trusts Prior to the Sherman Act," *Southern Economic Journal*, Vol. XXX (October, 1963), pp. 164–65.

[5] See, for example, Sidney Fine, *Laissez-Faire and the General Welfare State* (Ann Arbor: University of Michigan Press, 1964).

[6] See Joseph Dorfman's landmark work *The Economic Mind in American Civilization* (New York: Viking Press, 1949).

[7] Again, these chairs were usually multidisciplinary. For example, history and political economy were often coupled with some related area. Typical of the schools involved were Chicago, Johns Hopkins, Harvard, Yale, and Cornell.

The College and the Academic Department

The basic organizational unit in which the academic economist finds himself is the economics department.[8] Consisting of anywhere from a few to perhaps two dozen or more men, the department functions under a chairman or head who performs the general administrative tasks and reports to the dean of the college (or in a small college, to the president). The chairman usually recommends staff members for promotion, salary increases, tenure, termination, and in general "runs" the department. For these tasks, he receives a higher salary and a reduced teaching load. In some schools the chairmanship rotates among senior faculty members, while in other institutions the administrative duties are in the hands of an "executive officer" appointed on a yearly basis. In yet other cases, the chairman serves for an indefinite period.

A young economist going into academic life in the early 1970s will probably begin his or her career as an assistant professor, with a starting salary likely to be in the range from $8,500 to $12,500, depending upon such factors as location, type of school, and experience. For this salary, he is expected to teach nine months and to handle from two to four classes, depending on the school. That is, he must spend six to twelve hours in classroom contact per week, plus preparation and grading time and a modest amount of administrative work. As a young faculty member he may or may not have the opportunity to teach in his special field but generally must teach at least some survey courses or elementary economics. If he teaches in the summer session or evenings, he is compensated in addition to his nine months' salary. If he has not completed his dissertation or other Ph.D. work, he is expected to do so. If he has completed his degree, his seniors are likely to suggest that in order to progress he should publish on a modest scale, take some part in departmental committee work, and in general "pull his weight" in running the department.

If in the course of time the young faculty economist performs his duties satisfactorily, he can be expected to be promoted to associate professor (or to leave to accept such a post elsewhere). In the market of the 1960s the elapsed time from initial appointment to at least serious consideration for an associate professorship was not likely

[8] In a small college or community college, he may be in a more general department (e.g., the business department).

to exceed five years. Assuming a desire to stay in the field, the next
goal is, of course, the full professorship.[9]

Before World War II the rank of associate professor was often as
far as one might expect to go. Total enrollments were low, and outside opportunities were limited. The chance for promotion often
came only through the death or retirement of a senior faculty member, and as in the peacetime army of the 1930s, promotion was very
slow. Few could expect to become associate professors before the age
of forty and with at least fifteen years of experience. Most able men
in economics now can expect to reach full rank (somewhere) within
ten to fifteen years of starting. However, attaining this rank will
have increased the academic economist's salary surprisingly little.
Depending upon the man and the place, salaries for full professorships range from $17,000 to $30,000 (for 9 months), averaging
around $18,000 in the late 1960s.[10]

In pre-World War II years when professors were less mobile, the
department was a very close-knit unit, and the members were often
associates for many years. The modern department has, like the modern university, undergone changes and is now most often larger and
less cohesive.[11]

An economics department, like most, faces the continuous problem
of offering and staffing effectively two or more distinct programs of
study. Unless it is entirely a service department that provides only
basic courses as an adjunct to a narrow and specific major program
(as in some technical institutes and service academies), the department offers a broad program.

Almost every institution of higher learning offers a course in elementary economics. In junior colleges, small liberal arts colleges,
and technical institutes the course offering is likely to be restricted
to the elementary level, while a broader range of courses leading to

[9] While professor is the highest rank, there are endowed chairs, distinguished
professorships, etc., which embellish that rank with special honors or income
supplements. There are also research professors who seldom if ever teach but
who perform research, direct bureaus and projects, etc.

[10] Because of many divergent factors, "average" salaries are of little meaning
in academic life. See Francis M. Boddy, "Recent Behavior of Economists'
Salaries," *American Economic Review*, Papers and Proceedings, Eighty-second
Annual Meeting, American Economic Association, Vol. LXI, No. 2 (May,
1970), pp. 316ff.

[11] For the larger university issues see Jacques Barzun, *The American University* (New York: Harper and Row, 1968).

a major or to a graduate degree is available in larger institutions. In the 1962–63 school year, for example, 569 schools granted degrees in economics at the undergraduate level. However, the full range of work leading to the Ph.D. is found in a relatively small number of schools. Roughly seventy institutions (sixty-two in 1962–63) in the United States and Canada offer the degree, but their strengths and weaknesses vary widely.[12] Prestige schools, by and large, maintain at least a sprinkling of nationally known economists.

The fully staffed program serves at least two groups: economics majors who may or may not become professional economists, and general students who need or wish to take only the elementary courses. In addition, the graduate program has partially the same orientation. Specifically, graduate courses in economics are useful and open to graduate students in such fields as history, political science, and international affairs, as well as those who intend to become economists. As a result, the department provides the following services: (1) survey courses for many types of students throughout the institution; (2) more advanced and specialized courses for majors and non-majors; (3) graduate courses for majors and nonmajors; (4) Ph.D. level work directed almost entirely toward the professional economist; and (5) short courses, evening courses, etc., for various special groups and purposes. This broad program, of course, requires a wide variety of talents.

A typical, strong graduate program might offer most if not all the following fields of concentration:

> agricultural economics
> econometrics and statistics
> economic development
> economic history
> history of economic thought
> industrial organization
> international economic relations

[12] As noted, participation among schools is very uneven. Over the years, Columbia, California (Berkeley), Harvard, Johns Hopkins, Minnesota, Texas, and Wisconsin have been among the largest grantors of the Ph.D. degree in economics. Comparing schools is a hazardous hobby, but one writer considers the top five in economics to be Harvard, MIT, Chicago, Yale, and California (Berkeley). See Allan Cartter, *An Assessment of Quality in Graduate Education* (Washington, D.C.: American Council on Education, 1966).

labor economics and industrial relations
mathematical economic theory
price theory
public finance
public policy
theory of income, employment, and the price level
urban economics

Maintaining a faculty of sufficient distinction to man a Ph.D. program of this scope is a costly proposition, and the number of really first-class schools is thus limited. Teaching loads and resources for research must be favorable, and salaries must be high. A "respectable" offering might, of course, be undertaken with somewhat more modest resources. Top programs attract top students, and thus the advantage, once attained, tends to perpetuate itself. The same forces work in reverse when a failing program begins to be known and capable students shy away from it.

Relations between the department and the college or university are no different for economists than for other academics. In recent years economists have been in great demand in nonacademic areas, which has naturally enhanced their bargaining power; but this situation waxes and wanes. Historians, for example, were a glut on the market during the 1950s, were in great demand during the late 1960s, and were again in excess supply during the early 1970s. As the 1970s begin, economists appear to be in greater relative supply.[13]

When the economics department is located in the business school, there is often some hostility between economists and such specialists as accountants or marketing people because the economists often regard themselves as the "true scholars" and others as technicians. Also, the economists usually have close contact with liberal arts people and in fact are often listed in both colleges' faculties even though they "live in" the business school.

Stars, Super Stars, and Other Academic Types

In the world of academic economists there are perhaps two dozen "super stars"—men whose national reputations are so impressive that

---

[13] For a good discussion of the customs and mores of the academic trade see Theodore Caplow and Reece J. McGee, *The Academic Marketplace* (New York: Basic Books, Inc., 1958).

they would be welcomed on almost any university faculty and would increase the institution's reputation by joining it. Such scholars, usually prolific and respected writers, command top salaries and occupy endowed chairs.

These stars (or "name brand" economists) can often be divided into two types; those who emphasize academic excellence and have the professional respect of their associates, and those who are quasi-public figures, appear on "Meet the Press," "jet set" about the world, and may or may not have the professional respect of their colleagues. For example, Robert M. Solow (a super star himself) notes that John Kenneth Galbraith is a public figure "known and attended to all over the world," and that "he mingles with the beautiful people." Solow points out that Galbraith is someone special and that the more pedestrian economists hold him in awe and are to some degree envious.[14] Solow characterizes Galbraith as a "big thinker" whose ideas gravitate toward the direction in which the machine is going, while lesser economists devote their thoughts to the machine's parts. Galbraith is, of course, a unique man with many talents. Other super stars are more "economists' economists," highly respected within the ranks but totally unknown to laymen. For example, any university economics department would be delighted to hire one of the economists listed in Appendix A, but the general public would not know them. Thus a few super stars are public personalities while others remain within the confines of the profession. The total number in each category is of course small.

Stars of lesser magnitude come in greater numbers. Economists who have something of a national reputation within the profession and who have published a successful book or two might fit in this category. Stars operate on a more modest scale. While a super star may advise the president or win the Nobel Prize, the star may serve on a panel advising the secretary of commerce or win a prize of more limited distinction. Stars are less mobile, but the student who wishes to sit at the feet of a famous super star may be disappointed to find him on leave. For example, the 1970–71 bulletin of a famous university lists twelve super stars (out of seventy-two people) on its economics faculty; four of the super stars were on leave that year.

---

[14] "The New Industrial State, Son of Affluence," *Public Interest*, Vol. 9 (Fall, 1967). For some comments on the power structure by Galbraith himself see *Economics, Peace and Laughter* (Boston: Houghton Mifflin Co., 1971).

Both stars and super stars often teach only graduate courses, and some are research professors who never teach in the formal sense.

Organizations depend upon their journeymen, and universities are no exception. These faculty members are well trained, are generally hard working, and do the day-to-day work of classroom teaching, student advising, and committee work. In short, they "run the store." They also are more apt to constitute the department's permanent cadre, for the stars are likely to be more mobile.

Without able journeymen the department and the university would soon collapse. However, the journeymen sometimes justifiably feel that the stars and super stars (if the department has any in residence), are being overly paid and are promoted too rapidly. This view is sometimes shared by undergraduate students who may find journeymen more available and more compatible with their needs. Administrators and graduate students, on the other hand, enjoy "name dropping" the super stars and using the research funds they may attract.

John Kenneth Galbraith, pungent as usual, comments on the prestige system:

The prestige system of economics is wholly in accord with these principles. It assigns, and for good reason, the very lowest position to the man who deals with everyday policy. For this individual, in concerning himself with the wisdom of a new tax or the need for an increased deficit, is immediately caught up in a variety of political and moral judgments. This puts him in communication with the world at large. As such, he is a threat to the sharp delineation which separates the tribal group from the rest of society and thus to the prestige system of the profession. Moreover, his achievements are rated not by his professional peers but by outsiders. This causes difficulty in fitting him into the professional hierarchy and argues strongly for leaving him at the bottom.

A very low position is also assigned to economists who, even though forswearing any interest in practical affairs, occupy themselves with related disciplines—urban sociology, education, the social causes of poverty or juvenile delinquency. The reason is the same. These men are also inimical to the tribal delineation for their achievements depend on the judgment of noneconomists and thus cannot be integrated into the established scale. They are assumed by their colleagues to be escaping the rigors of their own subject.

At the higher levels, economics divorces itself fully from practical questions and from the influence of other fields of scholarship with the exception of mathematics and statistics. One can think of the full prestige structure of the subject as a hollow pyramid or cone, the sides of which, though they are transparent and with numerous openings at the base, become increasingly opaque and impermeable as one proceeds to the apex. Positions near the apex are thus fully protected from external communication and influence. Work here is pure in the literal sense.[15]

Extracurricular Activities

Outside activities—consulting, writing, and lecturing—play a major role in the professional lives of economists in academic circles, especially for the stars and super stars. Consulting to business firms or federal agencies has been popular in the past decade as the demand for such services expanded. Economists not only find this type of activity interesting but also a lucrative income supplement.[16] Most consulting takes the economist off the campus, but he may also engage in one of the many research projects carried out by the university (funded by federal agencies or foundations). Since 1950 it has been a rare faculty member who at some time in his career has not taken part in such an activity. A widely used rule of thumb allows a full-time faculty member to consult on the basis of one day per week, without raising serious questions about his real employer. If he has a nine months' teaching arrangement he may, of course, pick and choose from roughly the first of June until early September. Fees for such work vary widely depending on the fame of the economist and the type of work (court appearances, etc.). The "union scale" in the late 1960s probably was $150 to $200 per day.

Aside from its financial value to the professor, consulting is defended as a device to put the professor in touch with the real world while providing a service to the business community. It is attacked

---

[15] Galbraith, *Economics, Peace and Laughter,* pp. 38–39.

[16] The salary structures of teaching economists often contain supplementary income. Nonetheless, economists' salaries in general are somewhat depressed because so large a proportion of them are academics. Among university faculty members, however, economists' salaries rank well toward the top. Physical sciences and engineering are high, humanities generally low. See N. Arnold Tolles and Emanuel Melchar, "Studies of the Structure of Economists' Salaries and Income," *American Economic Review,* Supplement, Vol. LVIII, No. 5, Pt. 2 (December, 1968).

on the grounds that it becomes overly important, takes up excessive time, and often inhibits the professor from taking an independent position on issues of the day. These points, both good and bad, are often true. Most economists who have consulted value both the financial reward and the contact with the trade and in many cases would be reluctant to stop even if their salaries were raised to compensate for the loss in total income. A closely related activity which appears to be increasingly popular is appearing before congressional committees or consulting with senators and members of Congress on various economic issues. Academic economists, since they are not required to lobby, can often be more objective than their business or government counterparts when used in this capacity. Also, academic economists are often on the frontiers of work relevant to active issues (health economics, for example), and their testimony is valuable to the legislative process.

Writing

One hesitates to term professional writing an outside activity since it often is crucial to professional advancement and clearly is essential for recognition outside one's own institution. In large, research-oriented universities, promotion beyond associate professor (or even to associate in many cases), is difficult or impossible without having published. "Publish or perish" is sometimes the rule, although less often than is frequently said to be the case. A really outstanding classroom teacher is sometimes denied promotion because he has not published, but such cases are rare in most schools. One encounters the argument that writing and research enrich teaching, and conversely, that it is overdone to the detriment of teaching, especially on the undergraduate level. Students often denounce consulting and publishing with equal heat, for they naturally view the professor as teacher and often fail to realize that he not only "retails" scholarship but also "produces" it through scholarly research and writing. Both advancement and dissemination of knowledge are the scholar's functions. This is not to deny that market forces may tip the academic economist's scales too far in the direction of "productivity" and that an excessive amount of time may go into writing vis-à-vis classroom teaching in order to avoid "perishing." Many hours may be spent discussing the quality and scholarly content of Professor "A's" work. Is he a real scholar, a mere popularizer, or worst of all a "journalist"?[17] Whatever its intrinsic merit, publishing is a vital activity in academic life, and the possession of a long list of publications enhances a professor's market value more than any other single factor and no doubt outweighs several others in combination.[18]

Except in rare cases, a professor does not become rich by writing. Very popular elementary textbooks are big money makers, but only a few books reach this sales level (50,000 or more). Elementary economics is the only mass enrollment course in the field and has a national total of several hundred thousand students per year. In 1970 there were three major books in this area and perhaps a dozen others with smaller shares of the total market. The "big three" were clearly money makers on a large scale. In the more advanced courses with low enrollments, however, sales over the life of the book are apt to be no more than ten or twelve thousand copies. Of course, the competition a textbook faces in the mass enrollment courses is brutal, while one may have a monopoly in the specialized courses. In 1971 there were at least twenty books of various types available in elementary economics, but in special fields (for instance, transportation economics) there were only two or three. A common royalty figure is 15 percent; thus at $10.00 per copy (for new books only), the author nets $1.50, or a total of $18,000 for twelve thousand copies sold over perhaps a five-year period. This amount usually exceeds routine faculty raises, but most professors would be reluctant to work out the hourly wage. An advantage of writing over consulting, for example, is that once the book is written, income accrues without further effort as long as it can be sold. Furthermore, publishing is likely to win favor in the eyes of the university administration, and raises and promotions may even be attributed to writing.[19] However, even the mass enrollment texts are not in the same league with popular general books which may have sales of several million copies within months and salable movie and televi-

---

[17] This term is approximately equal in force to the term "photographer" applied by an abstract painter to a colleague whose work he finds too realistic.

[18] See, for example, Alexander Morin, "The Market for Professional Writing in Economics," *American Economic Review*, Vol. LVI, No. 1 (March, 1966), pp. 401sff.

[19] George Stigler has estimated that a major journal article in a prestige journal is worth between ten and twenty thousand dollars in increased lifetime earnings.

sion rights. Economists, like other professors, sometimes write detective stories or novels, truly extracurricular activities.[20]

The super star who has a public following may command substantial earnings from writing and lecturing. However, an economist who is also a public figure operates on a different level from his more pedestrian associates. Books or articles by these individuals are in the general market and occupy a status far different from the typical academic publication. Also, whereas the local Rotary Club is a forum for journeymen, the national lecture circuit is open to these figures at respectable fees.

Where Economists Come From

Large numbers of college students "major in" or take several courses in economics without ever intending to become professional economists. Most of these students enter business or law, become housewives, or pursue some other career. The number of students who major in economics but do not seek graduate degrees in the field is indicated in Table 1. Most professional economists now active and most of those now in training have formal education beyond the bachelor's degree. The completion of the Ph.D. is becoming increasingly important for full professional recognition, although this requirement was less common in the past, especially in government and business.

Students seldom have contact with economics as an academic subject prior to entering college. Although high schools are becoming increasingly aware of the importance of economics, it is still only rarely taught at the secondary level in a form similar to that on the college level.[21]

While slightly more than 15,000 undergraduate degrees were conferred in 1967–68, only about 2,000 master's and 600 doctor's degrees were earned. As in the field itself, numbers are small compared to other areas of study. For example, in 1967–68 almost 140,000

[20] The sale of several million books over ten or fifteen years is considered a legendary performance in academic life. While figures are not available, one might guess that Samuelson's elementary text has sold several million copies over twenty-two years.

[21] See, for example, "Economics in the Schools" (a committee report), *American Economic Review*, American Economic Association Supplement, Vol. LIII, No. 1, Pt. 2 (March, 1963). Much high school "economics" is still a mixture of civics, commercial education, and other subjects.

Table 1

Earned Degrees Conferred in the United States During 1967–68

Degree	Degrees in All Fields	Degrees in Economics[a]
Bachelor's	636,863	15,296
Master's	177,150	1,921
Doctor's	23,091	600

SOURCE: U.S., Department of Health, Education, and Welfare, *Earned Degrees Conferred*, Pt. A, 1967–68 (Washington, D.C.: Government Printing Office, 1968), OE–54013.
[a] Excludes agricultural economics.

undergraduate degrees were awarded in education (all fields), 23,307 in mathematics, almost 24,000 in psychology, and 20,000 in biology. On the Ph.D. level, economics with 600 compared more favorably, for Ph.D.'s in mathematics numbered 824 and biology only 314. Table 2 presents, in a more detailed form, these data for the past two decades.

Most fields have grown rapidly in recent years, and economics is no exception. In 1963–64, American institutions conferred 10,607 bachelor's degrees in economics and in 1967–68 granted 15,296. Doctorates rose from 368 to 600, with consequences that will be discussed later. Most fields showed much the same trend. For example, the number of bachelor's degrees granted in psychology and the number of doctorates conferred in education almost doubled. In the entire period from 1925 to 1935 only 1,166 Ph.D.'s in economics were granted, and only 1,317 were awarded during the next decade. By these standards, present figures are astronomical.

Obviously, only a small portion of those who major in the subject as undergraduates continue to the Ph.D. level. Economics seems to differ relatively little in this regard from other fields, as is shown in Table 3. One sees from these figures that in a number of fields few continue to the Ph.D. level and that the matter of employment orientation clearly is a factor. For example, the number of students who continue to the terminal degree in philosophy is much higher than in most of the fields noted. Surely this trend is due to the fact that undergraduate degrees in philosophy have very little direct "job potential" as compared, for instance, to a B.S. in mechanical engi-

Table 2

Bachelor's and First-Professional Degrees in Economics

Year	*Earned Degrees Awarded in Economics*[a]				
		Bachelor's[b]		Master's	
	Total	Men	Women	(2nd Level)	Doctor's
1947–48	9,002	7,684	1,318	922	116
1948–49	11,536	10,378	1,158	863	149
1949–50	14,573	13,471	1,102	921	200
1950–51	10,484	9,579	905	809	236
1951–52	8,595	7,520	1,075	695	239
1952–53	7,313	6,545	768	582	222
1953–54	6,728	5,938	790	609	245
1954–55	6,364	5,678	686	617	241
1955–56	6,938	6,259	679	753	293
1956–57	7,393	6,727	666	849	313
1957–58	8,142	7,535	607	933	310
1958–59	8,314	7,668	646	982	290
1959–60	8,101	7,422	679	995	313
1960–61	8,550	7,918	632	1,129	373
1961–62	9,111	8,344	767	1,217	379
1962–63	10,131	9,215	916	1,369	434
1963–64	11,385	10,311	1,074	1,449	500
1964–65	11,538	10,496	1,042	1,597	538
1965–66	12,274	11,130	1,144	1,901	586
1966–67	13,829	12,491	1,338	2,147	680
1967–68	16,207	14,569	1,638	2,358	752

SOURCE: USOE Earned Degrees Series. Also published in American Council on Education, *A Fact Book on Higher Education* (Washington, D.C.: 1969), p. 78.

[a] Includes economics and agricultural economics. The latter field was first identified separately in USOE reports for 1955–56.

[b] Includes first-professional degrees.

NOTE: Figures show degrees earned in colleges and universities in the U.S. and outlying parts during a twelve-month period ending June 30.

neering. Therefore, if a student aspires to be a professional philosopher, he must obtain the Ph.D.

Table 3

Bachelor's and Doctor's Degrees in Selected Fields, 1967–68

Field	Bachelor's	Doctor's[a]
Economics	15,296	600
Biology	20,941	314
Education	135,848	4,079[b]
Geography	2,624	96
Mathematics	23,307	824
Philosophy	4,161	261
Physics	5,045	1,260
Psychology	23,972	1,268

SOURCE: U.S., Department of Health, Education, and Welfare, *Earned Degrees Conferred*, Pt. A, 1967–68 (Washington, D.C.: Government Printing Office, 1968), OE–54013.

[a] One must, of course, recall that there is a time lag between the A.B. and the Ph.D.

[b] Ph.D. or D.Ed.

Most students who major in Arts and Sciences fields leave the higher educational process at the bachelor's level and in many cases enter a field to which the area of major interest might or might not be related. Economics at the undergraduate level is obviously not directed toward a specific career; or to put the matter another way, most people who major in economics as undergraduates have no intention of becoming professional economists.

It must also be noted that "majoring in economics" has no precise meaning on a universal basis. In major universities with strong departments the economics major is well defined in terms of economic theory, history, and other aspects of the field, and the student who follows it is well prepared for graduate study. In many small institutions, however, a major in economics is often actually a major in "general business" with a potpourri of accounting, marketing, and other courses not recognized as economics by prestige institutions.

Another factor related to entry into the profession is that practicing economists, unlike engineers, physicians, or salesmen, are rarely encountered by the average student. Small boys and girls may want to grow up to be lawyers, engineers, airline pilots, and nurses, but economists are generally invisible. The decision to become one is made at college age or at the bachelor's degree level. Very few people questioned in a street corner poll would be able to give the foggiest definition of what economists do or what training is required. This fact is supported by opinion surveys in which one-half or one-third of the respondents fail to recognize the term "economist" while they do recognize "college professor," "scientist," and similar terms. No doubt microbiologists and anthropologists would fare much the same. Since there are so few economists and they do not perform personal services in the usual sense, the chances of encountering one in the flesh are slim.

The survey course (usually six semester hours) at the sophomore level constitutes the first and often the last contact with formal economics for most college students, and they are most likely to discover economics and become interested at this point. Of course, a great majority of the students view the economics survey course solely as a task required or recommended by the field of study in which they are interested.

The student who wishes to become a professional must begin a graduate program leading eventually to the Ph.D.[22] When the student has completed this training period, he will have spent some seven to eight years in higher education and will probably be twenty-six to twenty-eight years old or older if he has had military service or has broken the period with a job. Normally, he will emerge with some special interest and will "sell himself" on that basis (he will be a labor economist, mathematical economist, money and banking

[22] The majority of students who begin this program of study fail to complete it. However, some of these do become professional economists. Most fail to complete the work because they do not finish the doctoral dissertation rather than because they lack ability in the technical sense. Those who do complete the full program may require a substantial period of time since it is common for students to leave the campus and pursue the dissertation while teaching or working elsewhere. For some specific data on these matters see Howard Bowen, "Graduate Education in Economics," *American Economic Review*, Supplement, Vol. XLIII, No. 4, Pt. 2 (September, 1953). These data are now old but are still generally valid.

man, theoretician, international economist, etc.). His area of special interest will have been formed not only by his experience, background, and courses taken but also by the research necessary to complete his dissertation.

For purposes of classification, the American Economic Association lists twelve specialties: general economic theory, economic history and history of thought, economic systems and planning, economic statistics, monetary and fiscal theory, international economics, business finance and administration, industrial organization (government and business, industry studies), land economics, labor economics, population and welfare, and "other." Many economists claim competence in two or more such areas. The largest number are in business finance and administration (a very broad field), and the smallest numbers are in population and welfare and "other."

There are, of course, many indices of competence as a specialist. An economist may have a mild interest in a field and may claim it for lack of any other, or he may have written half a dozen books in the field and have a national reputation as an authority. There are no formal qualifying examinations or accrediting groups similar to those in medicine to pass upon the individual's qualifications as a specialist.

Unlike his predecessors of the 1920s or 1930s, the new Ph.D. need not direct himself into academic life but can choose a career in government or business if he so desires. Thus more programs offering advanced degrees in economics are oriented toward business and government problems. Academic economists do more work in and have a better understanding of these areas than they did a generation ago, and they also are less hesitant to enter public affairs. Economists in most schools of thought are now more anxious to invade the forum of public policy, and even those who regard themselves as academics are less isolated from current affairs than they were some decades ago. As in many other academic fields, the classic "absent-minded professor" has become the "present-minded professor."

Most academic economists (and many others) belong to the American Economic Association. AEA is not a professional association in the strict sense. It has no professional requirements for admission— anyone who has an interest, the fee, and the endorsement of two members can join. It does not lobby for its members in the sense that the American Medical Association does, and it is in no way active as a "union."[23] Sole benefits of membership are receipt of two quarterly journals, the *American Economic Review* and the *Journal of Economic Literature,* and the right to attend the annual meetings. Annual meetings are devoted to the presentation of papers, business meetings, and the very important process of recruitment—the "slave market." Informally, as in most such rites, one renews acquaintances, promotes his books, attends receptions held by publishers, tries to hire or be hired, and in general participates in the typical convention.

Demand, Supply, and the Market Mechanism in the 1970s

Economists spend a rather substantial amount of time and effort examining their profession. They are, of course, professionally interested in demand and supply.[24]

The supply of economists was tight during the 1960s, and as is usual in a sellers' market, they enjoyed rising salaries, successively higher beginning salaries, and in other ways were generally in great demand. Ewan Clague estimated in 1962 that the supply of economists was apt to increase, and as the 1970s begin, this indeed has been the case.[25] In 1968 and 1969 the number of Ph.D.'s granted exceeded six hundred, roughly double the annual number at the beginning of the decade. Assuming that most recipients of the Ph.D. intend to enter the profession, which seems logical, can they be absorbed at rising salaries; or more precisely, what will be their impact on the market? As we will see, the demand has also increased as a result of the explosion in academic enrollments, the increase in the number of institutions, and also the growing opportunities in business and government. In view of this growth, the ways in which economists find jobs warrant some attention.

In general, due to the profession's small size and historical base in academia, the market for economists has always been satisfied in

[23] The organization most akin to a union is the American Association of University Professors. The AAUP is, of course, open to academics in general, including academic economists.

[24] See Ewan Clague, "The Market for Economists," *American Economic Review,* Vol. LII, No. 2 (May, 1962), pp. 497ff.

[25] "The Supply of Economists." Just how great this increase will be is a matter of debate. See the discussion "Round Table Session on the Academic Labor Market," *American Economic Review,* Papers and Proceedings, Vol. XLI, No. 2 (May, 1971), pp. 305ff. This discussion concentrates on the academic area and gives scant attention to the increasingly important business and government sectors of employment.

informal ways. Word of mouth, letters between department chairmen, friendly contacts, and other devices have been widely used in all areas of the market. The annual meetings of the American Economic Association have been a major marketplace for some years, both through the informal channels (prearranged meetings between job-seekers and recruiters) and through the more formal United States Employment Service, which registers and brings the parties together. Candidates nearing completion of their work make inquiries, write letters, and plan to attend the meetings. Relatively few people are placed through "want ads" in professional journals or in the mass media, and generally this method carries little prestige, as does employment via commercial placement agencies.[26]

The "in" schools generally use informal arrangements to hire faculty members and place their graduates, a practice that reflects the "clubbiness" of the profession. The "lesser" schools and their graduates are apt to use the formal machinery. This placement pattern has been followed by government and business, whose recruiters also attend the AEA meetings. Government economists tend to be recruited at lower levels by Civil Service announcements and at higher levels by personal contacts. No doubt, as the number of economists grows and the academic portion of the total market diminishes, methods will become more diverse. The current market mechanism leaves much to be desired. It is not very efficient for large numbers, and it leads to "inbreeding," as Gerald Somers notes:

If the current exchange arrangement between the largest graduate departments is to become the basis for a general center of market information, some means must be found to generalize it. One approach would be through an extension of the reciprocal trade agreements to an ever widening circle of universities. Some movement in this direction is already apparent with the recent admission of some smaller graduate departments into the cartel. Another approach would be through a liaison between the major graduate departments and the U.S. Employment Service. For the past several years the USES has maintained a roster of jobs and applicants at the AEA meetings. Although the agency has met with some limited success in obtaining applications for employment, orders from employers have been sparse. Analysis of applications, orders,

[26] See Gerald G. Somers, "The Functioning Market for Economists," *American Economic Review*, Papers and Proceedings, Vol. XLI, No. 2 (May, 1971), pp. 509ff.

interviews, and referrals for 1953 and the past four years reveals no trend toward the greater acceptance of the Employment Service. . . .

It is apparent that the USES roster presently lacks the prestige required for general acceptance by the economics profession. It is for this reason that a liaison between the Service and the major graduate departments would be essential for its wider utilization. To be successful, any public employment exchange for economists must develop under the principal aegis of the universities which provide the major crop of job applicants and the most sought-after job openings.[27]

Somers also feels that the prospects of great improvements in the market mechanism are not promising. Whatever its shortcomings, the current system has worked fairly well for professional economists, the Ph.D.'s (master's and bachelor's are in a different segment of the market).

By the end of the decade, the market had apparently shifted somewhat from its 1960 posture. While both demand and supply had increased, supply was beginning to match demand at the salaries being offered. The expansion in college economics enrollments had eased little if at all, but educational institutions were facing even greater demands in all areas and a growing reluctance from state and other sources to grant growing requests for funds. Likewise, "belt tightening" in various areas of the federal government had somewhat slowed the demand for economists in that area. These trends are likely to be temporary, but they currently have impact.

The effects of such changes are often peculiar and unpredictable. For example, the demand for graduate study often increases in such a period because students feel that they need to strengthen their competitive positions, and at the same time their outside opportunities are reduced. As salaries in industry and government level off and opportunities diminish, fellowships look better.[28]

By early 1970 the market had definitely softened. Departments with large Ph.D. programs were experiencing difficulties in placing

---

[27] *Ibid.*, pp. 516–18.

[28] Many economists who graduated from college in the early 1930s freely admit that they owe their graduate degrees to the fact that graduate stipends of a few hundred dollars per school year ($500 was common and $1,000 was untold wealth) plus fringe benefits were much more desirable than unemployment on the outside. Prizes of $10 to $25 (for the best essay on Simon Pattens' Economic Thought, for example) were much sought after.

graduates, especially in academic jobs where demand just four or five years before had seemed insatiable. Nonetheless, it is unlikely that demand will decline in the long run, and it should even increase. More and more complex issues hinge on economic analysis, and it seems likely that the economists' functions in business and government will expand over time. College enrollments will probably level off, but this should merely relieve the faculty shortage which has existed since 1950. The lag between demand and supply is, of course, substantial since several years must elapse between the decision to become a professional economist and actual entry into the market with a Ph.D.[29] On the other hand, the investment in time and money having been made, the new economist seldom leaves the field but enters under less favorable circumstances than he had anticipated. A frequent result of market glut is that the buyer upgrades his demands. Junior and community colleges, not able to attract many Ph.D.'s in the past decade, may demand and get them in the future, and the master's degree will slip further down on the totem pole. Informal soundings of the market during the past two years indicate that these forces are at work.

On Becoming an Economist

What characteristics render the economist unique? How does he differ from the engineer, the physician, or the chemist? What sort of student decides to enter the field professionally? One can speculate endlessly about these questions, and it is unfortunate that few data are available to answer them.

Limited data from the graduate record examinations and other sources indicate that economics graduate students' I.Q. scores and other indices of academic competence are near the average of students in other fields and are neither markedly lower nor higher than those of all students combined.[30] Basic intelligence is to be sure a requirement, though only one, for success in any professional field.

A list of mental and psychological characteristics which would be essential to success as an economist might include:

[29] This cycle makes forecasting difficult. An economist who received a Ph.D. in 1971, for example, was probably advised to go into the field in 1967 or 1968 when the market was good. His younger brother, advised in 1971 to avoid economics, may find in 1975 or 1976 that the market for new Ph.D.'s is excellent.

[30] Bowen, "Graduate Education in Economics," pp. 65ff.

1. A facility for abstract reasoning combined with a respect for the concrete (a rare combination of qualities). Many students find economics distasteful because it employs abstract reasoning. On the other hand, many who enjoy abstractions and who are stimulated by economic theory are unable to come "down to earth" and make sensible empirical observations. Also, many abstract thinkers have no "feel" for social and human problems which are, after all, the "stuff of economics."

2. An ability to think and reason logically. Economic interactions are involved and complex, and cause and effect may be difficult to separate. The successful economist must be able to think and reason clearly.

3. An interest in economic issues and a willingness to pursue such interests in depth. As we have seen, economic issues are broad and not readily separated from social and political matters. The successful economist must be willing to spend substantial time and effort in study and research.

4. A sense of history. Much of what will happen in the future has happened in the past. Interpreting economic events and keeping them in their proper perspective requires a sense of history and at least a working knowledge of it.

5. A sense of perspective regarding the application of knowledge. Since few economic problems yield to pure theory and few can be attacked entirely on the basis of empirical information, a combination of methodologies is essential.

6. The ability to write clearly. Most economic knowledge is, in the end, transmitted by the written word. A clear writing style is therefore a highly desirable quality.

7. A degree of professional detachment. The economist must be able to make an unemotional and detached analysis of issues. He does not need to refrain from involvement, but he cannot allow his emotions to overpower his analytical ability.

To sum up, the would-be economist, much like any other scientist, should be a scholar dedicated to his field and willing to work at it. Economists are men of their times. Those who have been attracted to the profession in every age have been concerned with the problems then current. Employment, stability, labor relations, and recovery were the active areas of interest for economists working in the 1930s. The post-World War II era stimulated much interest in international economic problems, while current interest is high in such fields as human capital, pollution, and the economics of poverty and discrimination.[31]

Kenneth Boulding notes that many people strongly believe that economists are indeed influenced by time and place and that the British-Western European origin of economics has been a major factor in its cultural development. He also observes that economics, like many other sciences, is dominated by those who are middle class or who tend to become so oriented. He suggests "awareness" as a remedy and argues that "culture-boundness" is most dangerous when it is unconscious.[32]

Complex and heterogeneous societies call upon everyone for a greater understanding and awareness of relationships. The academic economist cannot beg to be excused from this responsibility on the grounds of his scientific orientation. Economists have often been in the vanguard of social progress, and to a degree, the growth of the field has run parallel to increasingly difficult social problems. At times they have been in the forefront of efforts to more evenly distribute economic power and to diffuse the fruits of the economic system. Economists of all schools can justly claim some credit for the better understanding of socioeconomic relationships.

The Grand Awards

Every field has coveted honors that are awarded to members of distinction. While election to the presidency of the American Economic Association is not an honor per se and carries no pay or power, it is an obvious indication of high standing among one's fellows.

The AEA has two infrequently awarded medals of distinction, the Francis A. Walker Medal (awarded to those who have made outstanding contributions to the field) and the John Bates Clark Medal

---

[31] For many years the *American Economic Review* has printed titles of doctoral dissertations on an annual basis. These topics follow the trend of current thinking. Several written in the 1930s, for example, concerned the economics of relief.

[32] See Kenneth L. Boulding, "Is Economics Culture Bound?" *American Economic Review,* Papers and Proceedings, Eighty-second Annual Meeting, American Economic Association, Vol. LXI, No. 2 (May, 1970), pp. 406ff. For interesting comments, see William Breit and Roger L. Ransom, *The Academic Scribblers* (New York: Holt, Rinehart and Winston, 1971).

(awarded to economists under forty who have made outstanding contributions). The recipients are as follows:

Francis A. Walker Medal

1947—Wesley C. Mitchell
1952—John Maurice Clark
1957—Frank H. Knight
1962—Jacob Viner
1967—Alvin H. Hansen

John Bates Clark Medal

1947—Paul A. Samuelson
1949—Kenneth E. Boulding
1951—Milton Friedman
1953—No Award
1955—James Tobin
1957—Kenneth J. Arrow
1959—Lawrence R. Klein
1961—Robert M. Solow
1963—Hendrick S. Houthakker
1965—Zvi Grilches
1967—Gary S. Becker
1969—Marc Nerlove
1972—Dale Jorgenson

The Walker Medal is awarded once every five years and the Clark Medal every two years. The AEA also designates Distinguished Fellows (see Appendix A).

It is notable that the major awards of the profession still fall to those within the academic branch. No business or government economist has ever served as president of the American Economic Association, and every Walker and Clark medal has gone to an academic. Government economists have never been honored by the AEA except indirectly, as in the case of James Tobin, an academic economist who won the Clark Medal and later served on the Council of Economic Advisers.

The grandest prize of all, the Nobel Prize, was first awarded in economics in 1969 to Ragnar Frisch of Norway and Jan Tinbergen of the Netherlands. Both Frisch and Tinbergen, though academics and honored for econometric pioneering, were also active as government advisers. The 1970 award went to Paul Samuelson of MIT for his work in making economics more scientific. In 1971 the prize went to Simon Kuznets for his work in economic measurements, and in 1972 it was shared by the British economist Sir John Hicks (for work in general equilibrium theory) and Kenneth Arrow (for his work in welfare theory).

It can be imagined that the first Nobel prizes in the field were observed with close attention to the work selected.[33] One would expect academic economists to be dominant since most such awards are based on contributions to scholarship and published works, matters that are less likely to occupy the business or government economist.[34] Even in more worldly oriented fields, measures of professional renown are often based in academia. Distinguished engineers, businessmen, and lawyers are pleased to receive honorary degrees or membership in academic honor societies. Without knighthood or membership in the peerage to offer, Americans must be content with more modest kudos, and academic institutions have often been surrogate for the queen's honor lists.[35]

The academic economist plays many parts. He is teacher, researcher, writer, consultant, adviser, and often administrator. His unique and most meaningful role is that of teacher. Here he wields his greatest and longest-lasting influence. Yet this role has often been accorded the least prestige by the profession as the world of the economist has broadened. Before 1930 the economist's world was the academic world. By 1945 the government had opened to him, and by 1960 large numbers of economists had found their way into business. Many academic economists have, as we have seen, become involved in these areas while maintaining a base in academia. To a degree, this situation has brought both gains and losses. The academician, to the extent that he has involved himself in public issues

---

[33] See *New York Times*, 27 October 1970, p. 67.

[34] The NABE has established the Adolph G. Abramson Award to be given each year to the NABE member under thirty-five who is deemed to have made the most outstanding contributions. Established in 1968, it was first awarded in 1970 to Edward M. Gramlich of the Federal Reserve Board. For NABE-designated fellows, see Appendix A.

[35] Several notable British economists have been knighted, and Keynes became Lord Keynes, Baron of Tilton.

and in managerial problems, doubtless has become a more effective teacher.

Some 14 percent of all professional economists are employed by government, and for many years it represented the major area of endeavor other than teaching generally open to them. Let us examine the government economist.

4

The Government Economist

BEFORE 1920 only a handful of economists had penetrated the higher levels of government and had been given significant tasks involving professional economic analysis or advice. The First World War was a minor but temporary turning point since the hardheaded, laissez-faire orientation of the 1920s was, like the earlier years, not attractive to economists.[1]

The Era of Laissez-faire

Until well after the turn of the century federal involvement in the economy was at a minimum, and economists were neither needed nor generally interested in government participation. In general, the view was strongly held that the government should pursue a course of noninvolvement in the economy and that maximum freedom should be accorded to the individual. Though government had not been active in attempting to influence economic activity, it had upon many occasions acted to promote such areas as transportation and development of natural resources. These promotional activities were to continue even though the doctrine of laissez-faire, bordering almost on Manchesterism, had its day after the Civil War. Classical economic literature was dominant. Ricardo, Say, Smith, and Mill, as interpreted by their American counterparts and descendants, were generally accepted authorities, and the laws of political econ-

---

[1] This chapter draws on the author's book *The Role of the Economist in Government Policy Making* (Berkeley: McCutchan Publishing Corp., 1969).

omy were viewed as being as immutable as the laws of nature. The influence wielded by the historical school was also important.[2]

The historical school, powerful in academia, did not view activity in current public issues as part of its role. However, by 1870 this detached posture had come under increasing attack. The move against classical liberalism in the United States had a strong undercurrent of social or humanitarian philosophy. American thinking was greatly influenced by the desire for social justice and by the reform philosophies of pamphleteers and such book authors as Henry George and Edward Bellamy, whose works were read by millions. These "social justice" views were in sharp contrast to those of the "individualists" who were frequently products of the American frontier where a man often was able to rise in society through his own efforts.[3] The English philosopher Herbert Spencer and his American contemporary William Graham Sumner led those who accepted individualism, and it was fundamental in the legal structure as interpreted by the courts. In the East, however, where population was more dense and the industrial system had made greater headway, the doctrine of self-reliance began to be questioned.

Indeed, the gradual expansion of capitalism in the nineteenth century provided society with its most vexing problems. At first scattered and later more concentrated opinions that government power should be used to control this growing giant began to be heard. By 1880 the question of how and to what extent the commercial atmosphere should be controlled had moved to the center of the judicial stage, where it remained for some seventy years. As is usually true, these issues were essentially legal in nature and centered around interstate commerce, control of public utilities, minimum wages, and other socioeconomic matters.

However uneven the development of these legal-economic concepts has been, they increasingly have become the foundation of modern economic policy. The commerce clause, in particular, has grown far

[2] This school of thought was especially important in German-speaking nations and was largely a blend of romanticism, criticism of capitalism from the left, and a wide variety of social reform movements. For some forty years, beginning in the 1840s, it had considerable influence. See Eric Roll, *History of Economic Thought* (Englewood Cliffs, N.J.: Prentice-Hall, Inc., 1947), p. 331.

[3] See Fred Rodell, *Nine Men* (New York: Random House, Inc., 1955). This work traces the influence of individualism on the development of laws in business-government relations, especially on the Supreme Court level.

beyond what the founding fathers envisioned. This growth was not without considerable controversy, and the Court manfully struggled with these problems as the end of the nineteenth century approached.[4]

Laissez-faire was enthroned in the law, and Mr. Justice Holmes was able to complain only in vain that "the Fourteenth Amendment did not enact Mr. Herbert Spencer's Social Statics." The Supreme Court's view of laissez-faire is noted by Robert McCloskey as follows:

Their willingness to take to the ramparts on behalf of *laissez-faire* is made clear enough in the decisions involving the commerce clause. When the weapons were at hand the judges were ready to use them. In this field, it will be remembered, the Court had available the doctrine of federal pre-emption, drawn from such old decisions as Gibbons v. Ogden and Cooley v. Board of Wardens; and it was relatively easy to find state economic regulations invalid because they encroached on interstate commerce. The Court proceeded to do so in a series of decisions running in a seldom broken line from the year of Chief Justice Waite's appointment (1874) to the turn of the Century. The state's power to tax interstate business activity was seriously impaired in such decisions as the Philadelphia and Reading Railroad Case in 1873, which outlawed freight tonnage taxes on interstate shipments; and other state attempts to control business within their borders fell under a similar ban in the 1870's. Perhaps the most important of these early decisions was the Pensacola Telegraph Case in 1877 which precluded the states from granting telegraph monopolies but it is only one of several. The rise of the regulatory movement was bringing commerce cases to the Court in growing numbers, and the judges were giving notice that state laws in this field would be scrutinized with a sharp eye.[5]

Despite judicial reluctance, the reaction against established institutions grew in strength after 1880, and by 1900 both the "new school" economists, many of whom had been trained in Germany, and the

---

[4] This clause, which underlies much regulatory legislation, reserves to the federal government the power to regulate commerce between the states, foreign nations, and Indian tribes. Intrastate commerce can be regulated by the states. Broadly interpreted, this concept covers all business enterprise but the most trivial and is a very potent regulatory device. See Hugh S. Norton, *Economic Policy: Government & Business* (Columbus: Charles E. Merrill Publishing Co., 1966), pp. 54ff.

[5] *The American Supreme Court* (Chicago: University of Chicago Press, 1960), p. 124. © 1960 by the University of Chicago, published 1960. The Chicago History of American Civilization, Daniel J. Boorstein, Ed. Printed in the USA.

"institutional economists" were raising fundamental questions about the system as it operated. However, it is fair to say that in these years economists were not directly influential in public affairs as economists, with perhaps the exception of some institutionalists whose intellectual heirs were in the forefront of the reforms stemming from Woodrow Wilson's New Freedom. Their students were to reappear two decades later in the ranks of the New Deal.[6]

The lack of rapport between the academic economists and their popular lay colleagues such as Henry George was symbolic of the split between the groups. The institutional economists came closer to applying economics to social problems since they rejected the idea that laissez-faire was an automatic and infallible guide to economic action. This school made no attempt to discover scientific "laws" similar to those of the physical sciences because in their view such activity was fruitless.[7] Thus they generally alienated themselves from their academic fellows who adopted the "scientific" approach and steered clear of practical problems.

The institutional economists were trailblazers into public life, for they were interested in moving into government and taking part in its affairs. Their careers also illustrate clearly one of the reasons why relatively few academic economists were willing to follow in their footsteps. Specifically, such actions generally involved the academic institution as well as the economist in controversial situations. John R. Commons and Richard T. Ely were forced to resign several academic positions because of their outspoken views on social issues of the day, particularly labor relations. Thorstein Veblen, even more outspoken and also unconventional in his personal conduct, was never secure and never rose beyond the rank of assistant professor.[8]

[6] In *The Age of Roosevelt: The Politics of Upheaval,* Vol. 3 (Boston: Houghton Mifflin Co., 1953), Schlesinger notes that many of the early New Deal figures were influenced as students by the institutionalists.

[7] See Ben B. Seligman, *Main Currents in Modern Economics: Economic Thought Since 1870* (Beverly Hills: Free Press of Glencoe, 1962).

[8] In 1924, five years before his death, Veblen was elected president of the AEA but declined the honor, noting that it was too late to be of professional aid. Veblen not only questioned established business practices but was often involved in amorous adventures, a fatal combination in the years before 1930. He was the original "economist-hippie," smasher of idols and a trial to the university establishment. See Max Lerner, ed., *The Portable Veblen* (New York: Viking Press, 1948); and Joseph Dorfman, *Thorstein Veblen and His America* (New York: Viking Press, 1934).

Nonetheless, these men led the profession into the public forum. In discussing one of these leaders, Daniel Fusfeld notes:

> Underlying Commons' ideas was a philosophy of government that placed the state in the role of mediator between conflicting economic interests and between economic forces and the individual. Commons and other liberal reformers saw conflicts of interest, which had to be resolved with fairness to both sides, between business and the public, between labor and management, and, in broader terms, between the free operation of market forces and individual welfare. This view of conflict differed sharply from those maintained by the other two chief ideological positions—from that of the neoclassical economists, who saw harmony emerging in all areas out of the equilibrating forces of the market, and from that of the Marxists, who argued that class conflict would inevitably tear the social order apart. Commons accepted both of these concepts but went beyond them; he argued that market forces could reconcile some but not all of the conflicting interests of the modern world and that a complex industrial society continually created new conflicts whose equitable resolution required government action.
>
> The reforming, social welfare philosophy expressed by Veblen and the policies pioneered by Commons and his associates came to fruition during the 1930's under the New Deal administrations of Franklin D. Roosevelt, when the concept of the welfare state became dominant. It is true that old ideas began to change before the thirties: witness the welfare legislation of New York and Wisconsin, the conservation movement prior to World War I, and the gradual acceptance by government of the use of monetary policy to promote economic stability.[9]

Commons was the most active in the real world, and during his years at the University of Wisconsin, he immersed himself in practical affairs. According to Ben Seligman:

> There were many opportunities to observe political behavior at Wisconsin. Commons became an advisor to Robert La Follette, the State's exciting and forward-looking governor, who was anxious to undertake a wide variety of social reforms. Commons plunged into a mass of work. He helped draft a civil service bill in 1904; pushed public utility regulation in the municipal area; promoted a small-loan law which allowed a charge of 3½ percent interest a month (for which he was attacked even though 42 percent per annum was a good deal less than a 100 percent

---

[9] From *The Age of the Economist* by Daniel R. Fusfeld. Copyright © 1966 by Scott, Foresman and Company. (p. 94)

interest charge) ; helped create the Wisconsin Industrial Commission; and in 1932 turned out one of the first state unemployment insurance measures in the country. He was also involved in studies of municipal ownership; the Pittsburgh Survey of 1906; the Federal Industrial Relations Commission of 1913; and the famous Pittsburgh plus-pricing case of 1923. He was America's closest challenge to the indefatigable Webbs.

Ultimately all this experience went into the creation of the peculiar system of thought exemplified in the *Legal Foundations of Capitalism and Institutional Economics*. His unique ability for gaining the confidence of all sorts of people, from radical socialists to staid millionaires, enabled him to explore varying human situations. Despite personal tragedies—the loss of five children, and a sixth who suffered from paranoia, as well as his own poor health—he maintained a remarkable equanimity. Toward the end of his life, he felt that his last book, *The Economics of Collective Action*, finally had made clear to the profession what it was he had been trying to tell them for so many years.[10]

Thorstein Veblen was not alive to see his ideas put into practice, but as Seligman points out:

It can be fairly said that a Veblenian school of economics did in fact develop, but it did not last. The Veblenians were in their early thirties when the master died and they were soon caught up in day-to-day problems, particularly in New Deal affairs. With a depression and a war, they had to improvise policies after the fashion of their great political godfather—Franklin Delano Roosevelt. Each Veblenite took up a different facet of the many-sided institutionalist analysis. Some, as in the case of Walton Hamilton, became interested in legal matters, while others sought more empirical data, and after a while eschewed theory altogether. This, in a sense, was ironic, for Veblen himself had demonstrated that little could be gained by an everlasting ingathering of facts without theory. Yet Veblen's influence has regrettably waned. The Keynesian revolution in economics and the explosive development of the mathematical approach in the forties and fifties shunted aside the genetic viewpoint. Lip service was paid to the problems of the group, as in game theory, but it was seldom done with the plasticity and variability that one finds in the real world.[11]

[10] Ben B. Seligman, *Main Currents in Modern Economics: Economic Thought Since 1870*, p. 158. Copyright 1962 by The Free Press of Glenco, a division of The Macmillan Company. For information write: The Free Press of Glenco, a division of The Macmillan Company, Crowell-Collier Publishing Company, 866 Third Ave., New York, N.Y. 10022.

[11] *Ibid.*

Richard T. Ely, like Commons, was active in affairs off campus and served on various commissions, boards, and other public policy bodies. Other academic economists concerned with public matters were E. R. A. Seligman, whose main interest was in taxation, and Thomas Nixon Carver, who did pioneering work in distribution theory. Finally, W. C. Mitchell of Columbia University did yeoman work on price problems during the First World War. Mitchell was again called upon to use his skill during the 1930s.

This experience strengthened his belief in the need for planning. This was the nation's most important and most difficult task. But whatever else it was, insisted Mitchell, it was not un-American. Planning, he reminded his readers, could be found in the Articles of Confederation, Hamilton's scheme for a new economic system, and in wartime programs for mobilization. In a talk to the economics club at Columbia in 1941, he again stressed the importance of factual knowledge for planning. While he did not dismiss theory, he expressed greater preference for the fact economist as against the word economist. "In formulating economic policies to meet the present emergency," he said, "we shall find the empirical knowledge acquired by our science of inestimable value." But, he continued, "to get the most out of this knowledge we must use it analytically. That is, we must work as theorists with the data at our disposal."[12]

Despite these individual advances, interest in policy matters within the profession was still restricted to a relatively small group at the turn of the century. Nonetheless, public regulation of business was a very active issue from 1890 to 1914, reaching a peak with Woodrow Wilson's New Freedom. Not until the New Deal era did a similar wave of economic reform take place. Academic economists, however, were not in the forefront of this movement, and in fact they remained largely cloistered.

Wilson's New Freedom perished in the First World War and was followed by a return to laissez-faire in the 1920s. The disturbing years of the 1930s were instrumental in changing economists' outlook toward participation in practical politics, and as a consequence, economists of all schools of thought began to abandon their long-held belief that the economist should be merely an observer and never a participant in affairs of state.

[12] *Ibid.*

The Pioneers

The First World War was a marked though temporary turning point during which a number of economists entered federal service. Irving Fisher devoted his presidential address to the American Economic Association in 1918 to a discussion of these new opportunities. Nonetheless, the presence of some economists in federal service did not prevent the severe economic problems of total war during the 1940s. No serious attempt was made to ration goods or to control output on a broad basis; no concept of the relationship of the aggregate economy to the war effort was formulated. Consequently, little economic analysis in the modern sense was required. At the end of the First World War, most economists in federal service returned to their academic pursuits and remained there until the New Deal years. The foundation for the economists' present prominence in government circles was laid during the Second World War.

It might be noted in passing that the participation of economists in the British government has always been significant. Since the days of Malthus, British academic economists have served in influential advisory positions. One might suspect that the British experience has had some impact upon the American situation, especially during and after the Second World War.[13]

In the early New Deal era the economist became a standard, though controversial, fixture in Washington. The early brain trusters—Raymond Moley (a political scientist), Adolf Berle (a lawyer), and Rexford Tugwell and Gardiner Means (economists)—were often

---

[13] For a good picture of how the academic economist divided his time and talents between the university and Whitehall, see Roy Harrod, *Life of John Maynard Keynes* (New York: Harcourt, Brace, & World, 1951). See also Robert Hall, *The Place of the Economist in Government*, Oxford Economic Papers, No. 7 (June, 1955), pp. 119–35; A. K. Carincross, "On Being an Economic Advisor," *Scottish Journal of Political Economy*, No. 2 (October, 1955), pp. 181–97; P. D. Henderson, *The Use of Economists in British Administration*, Oxford Economic Papers, No. 13 (February, 1961), pp. 5–26; J. M. D. Little, "The Economist in Whitehall," *Lloyds Bank Review*, No. 44 (April, 1957), pp. 29–40; Ely Devons, "The Role of the Economist in Public Affairs," *Lloyds Bank Review*, No. 53 (July, 1959), pp. 26–38; Graham Hallett, "The Role of Economists as Government Advisors," *Westminster Bank Review* (May, 1967), pp. 67–81; and Gerhard Golm, letter to Gert von Eynern, *Interdependensen von Politik und Wirtshaft* (Berlin: Festgabe fur Gert von Eynern, Duncker & Humbolt, July, 1966), pp. 309–16.

in the news.[14] Yet their influence was less as pure economists than as general advisers. It is likely that Roosevelt's experience with neoclassical economists had convinced him that they were unable to give helpful technical assistance. The economists in power during the early Roosevelt years were, for the most part, descended from the founders of the institutionalist school of economics. Although Gruchy attributes great influence to this group as policy makers, it is likely that they exerted more influence as "social architects" than as economists in the technical sense. This group was never clearly defined, and its membership was largely a matter of newspaper speculation. Raymond Moley complained that anybody who had a college degree and a briefcase was, in newspapermen's eyes, a brain truster. The group dominated by academics and writers was looked upon with scorn by the conservative press and was widely distrusted by the business community.

The brain trusters' activities certainly ranged far beyond the collection and interpretation of economic data. In fact, there is little evidence that FDR relied on these men for economic advice per se. If he found little help from the neoclassical economists, he apparently found only a modest amount of usable material in the early ideas of Keynes, as Seymour Harris indicates. However, Alvin Hansen, Keynes's leading American disciple, was a powerful force in New Deal circles, and the Keynesian thesis had a fundamental influence upon New Deal economics.[15]

The New Deal had many economic facets, and it is unnecessary to discuss them here. One major problem was that the program was made up of many diverse parts which often overlapped and sometimes conflicted.

[14] One source attributes the term "brains trust" to Franklin P. Adams. See Arthur Krock, *Memoirs: Sixty Years on the Firing Line* (New York: Funk and Wagnalls, 1968). However, in *The Brains Trust* (New York: Viking Press, 1968), Rexford Tugwell claims that it was invented by Walter Kirnan of the *New York Times*. In his book, *Working with Roosevelt* (New York: Harper and Row, 1952), Samuel I. Rosenman describes his suggestion to Roosevelt that such a group be established and implies that FDR was attracted by a novel idea. Actually, the idea may not have been so new to FDR as Rosenman thought. Roosevelt's mentor, Al Smith, had as governor of New York made calls on academic talent. See Matthew and Hanah Josephson, *Al Smith: Hero of the Cities* (Boston: Houghton Mifflin Co., 1969).

[15] See, for example, Eliot Janeway, *The Economics of Crisis* (New York: Weybright and Tally, Inc., 1968); and Lekachman, *The Age of Keynes*.

New Deal economists, whatever their contribution in Washington, were an anathema to conservative businessmen and the press. Perhaps the prototype of brains trusters, and certainly the one who was most bitterly criticized, was Rexford G. Tugwell, the epitome of the "radical" economist of his era.

Tugwell, a young Columbia economics professor, was known as "Rex the Red." Labeled a Communist and depicted in the *Chicago Tribune* as a foolish figure in academic garb offering ridiculous advice to wise men, he became the whipping boy of the administration. Tugwell was brilliant, arrogant, handsome, and had little patience with most senators and congressmen, whom he considered to be his mental inferiors (and who often were). Patrick Anderson describes the situation which resulted:

> It was Tugwell's advocacy of consumers' interests that first inspired widespread criticism of him. With Roosevelt's approval, he had a new Food and Drug Act written and sent to Congress in June 1933. This legislation, soon dubbed the Tugwell Act, set high standards for the labeling and advertising of drugs. It vigorously opposed, someone commented, the God-given right of free enterprise to sell horse linament as a cure for cancer.
> The problem was that Tugwell had no political sense. His boss at Agriculture, Wallace, was no better off, and Roosevelt was too busy to worry about the timing and presentation of a food and drug bill. Tugwell's first blunder came even before his bill was introduced. He issued an administrative order reducing the maximum amount of poisonous-spray residue allowable on fruits and vegetables. Immediately fruit growers protested to their Congressmen, and resistance to the Tugwell Act began to stiffen even before it reached Congress. . . .[16]

Tugwell's enemies found an abundance of ammunition to use against him in his own voluminous writings. They joyously unearthed (and had read on the Senate floor) a woeful, Whitmanesque poem he had written in college. The newspapers gave extensive coverage to charges by a Dr. William Wirt, school superintendent in Gary, Indiana, that Tugwell was the leader of a revolutionary plot within the government. As Dr. Wirt explained it to a rapt congressional

---

[16] Patrick Anderson, *The President's Men* (Garden City: Doubleday and Co., Inc., 1968), p. 34. © 1968 by Patrick Anderson. Doubleday and Co., Inc. Garden City, N.Y., 1968.

committee, the plotters were using Roosevelt as a Kerensky, but Tug-well was soon to emerge as the Lenin of a Red dictatorship in America.[17]

Tugwell was from time to time removed to the background when FDR felt that he would be embarrassing. Later in his career he was made governor of Puerto Rico and in 1945 returned to teaching and writing. Of all the New Deal economists, Tugwell suffered the most, for in many ways he was symbolic of New Deal economics to anti-Roosevelt groups.[18]

The government economist was regarded at best as the archetypal "do good" planner who "never met a payroll" and interfered with legitimate business. (Bernard Baruch defined him as a man with a Phi Beta Kappa key on his watch chain, without a watch.)[19] Though the profession as a whole made a positive contribution, in some cases charges of arrogant interference were not entirely untrue; and it cannot be denied that the economist (like everyone else) failed to find a ready solution to the depression. Despite whatever place he had carved out for himself in the federal establishment, the econo-mist found his reputation in the business community at low ebb by the time the Second World War began. His stock was not much higher in the Congress, which had, for example, abolished the Na-tional Resources Planning Board in 1944 and was far from unani-mous about the merits of the Employment Act of 1946.[20]

Several points must, however, be made in defense of the profes-sion's performance. In the first place, the "economists" who waxed fat in these years were either poorly trained or not trained at all in formal economics. Several were lawyers, others were businessmen or

[17] Anderson, *The President's Men*, p. 35.

[18] See Bernard Sternsher, *Rexford G. Tugwell and the New Deal* (New Brunswick: Rutgers University Press, 1956). Tugwell tells his own story in *The Brains Trust*.

[19] See Rosenman, *Working with Roosevelt*, pp. 56ff.; and Schlesinger, *The Age of Roosevelt*, pp. 189ff., and "The Keynesian Revolution and Its Pioneers," *Proceedings*, American Economic Association, Vol. LVII, No. 2 (May, 1972), pp. 116ff.

[20] See Edwin G. Nourse, *Economics in the Public Service* (New York: Harcourt, Brace & World, 1955) ; and Stephen Kemp Bailey, *Congress Makes a Law* (New York: Columbia University Press, 1950). When Nourse set up the CEA in 1946, he avoided the old NRPB quarters for fear of association with that body in the congressional mind. Keynes' role in these years is detailed in Lekachman, *The Age of Keynes*, especially Chapt. 5.

journalists, and at least one was an historian.[21] Let us keep in mind that these men obtained their formal educations before 1920, the period when academic economics was a very heterogeneous field of study. Though capable men, none of them were of the caliber of the present-day leaders on Council of Economic Advisers as economists. Furthermore, under FDR's well known mode of operation, none of them were engaged in economic analysis or advice per se. Rather, they ranged far and wide as planners or "social engineers" with only vaguely defined tasks. When kept within their professional competence they did reasonably well. Also, they were working with inadequate data. In fact, one of the major contributions made by the pioneer federal economists was the assembly of systematic statistics.

Finally, the New Deal was by no means sold on Keynesian economics; and until the war years, budget deficits remained too small to be effective in fiscal policy and too large to give businessmen confidence in the administration. Early efforts to implement effective Keynesian economics were subject to great debate both at the time and afterward. Not until the Kennedy-Johnson years three decades later would the New Economics come into its own. Relatively few of the data now available had been collected before 1935, and the economists' tool kit was poorly stocked. However, these mitigating circumstances were neither known nor of great interest to the business community, which remained fully convinced that the economists' natural habitat was the classroom. It seems likely that by the time the Second World War began, the prestige of economists as practical men of affairs had reached an all-time low. However, changes were beginning even in those bleak years.

Moley, Tugwell, and their New Deal associates were political economists interested in social reform and political development. Their basic ideas were close to those of Wilson's New Freedom. When the Second World War began, men with experience in industry came into power in Washington; the hard goods of war replaced the soft goods (ideas) current between 1933 and 1939. Many serious eco-

---

[21] The "brains trust" was never well defined and changed from time to time. Typical members were Raymond Moley, a political scientist; Adolf Berle, a lawyer; Rexford Tugwell and Lauchlin Currie, economists; Charles Beard, an historian; and Hugh S. Johnson, an army officer and lawyer who headed up the NRA.

nomic problems had to be faced at once, and a new breed of economist trained during the years of the Keynesian revolution was called upon. These younger economists, more specialized and better trained than the political economists and journalists of the Roosevelt era, have come to the fore in recent years. The reasons for their rise will be considered in a later chapter.

When the Second World War began, the agencies concerned with mobilization proliferated rapidly. A large number of economists were called from academic pursuits to take over tasks in such wartime agencies as the Office of Price Administration, the War Production Board, the Office of Strategic Services, and the Board of Economic Warfare. Also, a number of economists who had already made a reputation in government were recruited to man these agencies temporarily. After the war ended, other temporary and generally short-lived organizations were established and operated under similar conditions. However, some "temporary" wartime service lasted for years.

Most of the economists in the wartime agencies did a workmanlike job; but under the circumstances, only a relative handful were in really significant positions, and few were able to wield long-term influence. Some, such as Leon Henderson (who directed the Office of Price Administration), had been notable figures in the early New Deal years; but others, including Walter Heller and Gardner Ackley, were at an early stage in their careers. Many economists now in middle age had just completed their professional training at this time, and unlike their older associates, they often began their careers in federal service. Many have spent two or three different terms in federal service, returning to academic life in the interims. Gardner Ackley, for example, was in wartime Washington, returned to the University of Michigan, served as a CEA member and chairman in the mid-1960s, was ambassador to Italy until 1970, and again returned to Ann Arbor and academic pursuits. Interestingly enough, few go into high-level business. While some join foundations or research groups, most return to the campus. For example, in 1970, twenty former CEA members were living. One was retired, two were back in government, two were in business, fourteen were in academic life, and one was with a foundation.

It is difficult to say just how many economists in federal service would be accepted as professionals by their colleagues in other areas.

Those in high-level positions are, of course, very conspicuous; and it is quite likely that their overall importance may be somewhat distorted by the radiance of those in the Council of Economic Advisers and other posts of great influence and high visibility. Ackley, former chairman of the council, noted recently:

Today, economists by the hundreds are employed in the Federal Government. The present Director of the Bureau of the Budget—like his two predecessors—is a distinguished economist, so are and have been the last four incumbents as Assistant Directors of the Bureau. The Under Secretary of the Treasury for Monetary Affairs and his immediate predecessor are professional economists, as are the Assistant Secretary of Treasury for International Affairs and the Under Secretaries of Agriculture and Health, Education, and Welfare. The second of two professional economists now serves in the recently created post of Assistant Secretary of Commerce for Economic Affairs. Four members of the Board of Governors of the Federal Reserve System are professional economists, as are the Presidents of a number of the Federal Reserve Banks. A number of first-rate economists have helped turn the Pentagon upside down in the past five years. Several professional economists hold or have held major ambassadorial posts as well as Assistant Secretaryships in the Department of State. AID has become an economist's preserve. Both the Treasury and the Federal Reserve have Consultant Groups consisting of distinguished professional economists, whose policy advice is frequently and eagerly sought. More than one economist in private life has survived the shock of finding the President of the United States at the other end of his telephone line. The Council of Economic Advisers finds—sometimes to its regret—that it has no monopoly on professional economic advice in the formation of Administration economic policy.[22]

Most of the hundreds of whom Ackley speaks labor without being widely known and have little influence outside their own immediate circle.

The *National Register of Scientific Personnel* referred to earlier indicated that 1,274 economists in the federal government met *NRSP* standards and thus would be considered professionals. Therefore, some 1,200 economists with sound professional qualifications were employed on the federal level in 1964, although various criteria might be used which would greatly increase the total number.

[22] "Contribution of Economists to Policy Formulation," *Journal of Finance,* Vol. XXI, No. 2 (May, 1966), p. 170.

Recent data are of interest. A Civil Service Commission publication, *Occupations of Federal White Collar Workers,* indicates that a total of 4,451 persons classified as economists were employed by the federal establishment.[23] Although standards have been raised in recent years, the Civil Service definition of an economist traditionally has been quite liberal and is still more liberal than the National Science Foundation definition since the Civil Service Commission list of economists is more than triple the 1,200 included three years earlier in the *NRSP*. Opportunities obviously have not increased threefold during the intervening period. Of these, the greatest number (1,073) were in the State Department, and 927 were in Agriculture. Commerce had 414, Treasury included 187, and agencies not separately listed accounted for 386. Several agencies had only a handful (the Post Office had 24 and the Navy had 3), while the Atomic Energy Commission had a single individual. No criteria for appointment were given. In addition, 89 "economics assistants" were employed but were not described. For comparison's sake, the same publication indicates that the federal establishment employed 12,396 engineers and 9,447 lawyers.

More than half of the federal economists were located in the Washington, D.C., area. While 2,149 were men, only 386 were women. Men had a median grade of GS-13 and an average salary of $15,388, while women had a median grade of GS-12 and an average salary of $12,418. Overall, the average grade was GS-13 and the average salary $14,935.[24] No breakdown showing areas of specialization or educational data were given.

The *NRSP* registered a total of 12,143 economists, of which 41.9 percent were reported to have the Ph.D. degree. Of the 1,274 in federal employment, 450 were reported to have the Ph.D. degree, while 254 had a bachelor's degree or less. Thus roughly one-third of the government economists held a Ph.D., but almost three-fourths of the economists employed by educational institutions were so qualified. Government economists' experience is frequently limited by a high degree of specialization, while Civil Service status and liberal federal retirement make them relatively immobile. Also, in

[23] U.S., Bureau of Manpower Information Systems, *Occupations of Federal White Collar Workers,* USCC Statement SM–56–7 (Washington, D.C.: Government Printing Office, 1967).

[24] *Ibid.,* p. 44.

recent years federal salary levels have risen to the point where they would be unlikely to match their earnings (given their training) in academic life. Large numbers of them have done substantial work toward the terminal degree but have never completed it, in most cases foundering at the dissertation stage and remaining "ABDs" (all but dissertation). No doubt the expanding opportunities for economists in government since the early 1940s have lured many Ph.D. candidates away from their studies. These rank and file economists, though often the workhorses of their agencies, seldom receive top billing.

These economists' tasks vary widely depending, of course, upon the nature of the organization and its mission. The USDA is clearly concerned with the welfare of agriculture; yet interpreted liberally, this is a broad hunting license. Economists in the department concern themselves with the marketing of agricultural commodities, rates for transporting agricultural commodities, relocating farmers, and many other issues which would not generally occur to the casual observer. Since each agency is generally anxious to expand its role, the number of related matters is constantly growing. Also, new programs have in recent years presented new challenges and opportunities to federal economists in most departments, and this trend seems likely to continue. These forces have demanded not only more economists but better economists with more adequate and specialized training.

While the academic economist must (if he is to progress) write books or articles, the federal economist has only to do his immediate job, although the few who do publish are not likely to be disadvantaged professionally by doing so. Since higher ratings mean more money and status and often involve administration, the Civil Service economist may become more of an administrator than an economist. Quite frequently a promotion converts a good researcher into a poor administrator.

Employees whose expertise is in other fields but who perform some type of economic analysis or related work are often classified as economists, frequently a catchall term. Some realignment began in the mid-1950s with greater weight being put on professional training. However, large numbers of long-term civil servants who have no reasonable qualifications still bear the title of economist. Those with legal and statistical training, for example, are sometimes classed as economists, as are those senior clerks who, though capable in some areas, have no professional training of any type.

The most serious shortcomings of the Civil Service economist are his frequently narrow training and his emphasis on empirical background. Often known by such titles as agricultural economist, transportation economist, and industrial economist, he reflects the interest of his agency. Working full time on a narrow range of problems, his outlook as well as his expertise becomes parochial, particularly if he lacks sound professional training. This is not to imply that he is not capable and valuable to the organization. He often accumulates a tremendous amount of empirical information, has contacts with those in the field, and in other ways makes himself very useful. However, his great value is more often as a general "know-how" man than as an economist per se.

Most of these people do a satisfactory job (often a very superior job) since they are, in many cases, highly experienced and have specialized information at their fingertips. Unfortunately, they lack the breadth of training and professional orientation which they would have acquired by systematic study in the field.[25] Thus a "transportation economist" employed by the Bureau of Public Roads (likely a civil engineer by training), may be very knowledgeable about highway economics, but his general economic knowledge and hence his ability to communicate with fully trained economists and to relate his information to the whole field is sharply limited. Many "economists" engaged in numerous tasks throughout the government would be excluded from the ranks of professional economists by most reasonable standards. Most of them labor unsung. Their roles are not influential; yet they perform a useful function. As time passes and professionalism within the field increases, they will probably be reclassified; and to some extent this process is already in motion.

[25] Professionals in the Civil Service are appointed on the basis of an "examination" (i.e., completing of a personal history upon which the candidate indicates his training, experience, etc.) This form is then rated by the Civil Service with points assigned for each category. Historically, practical experience has counted heavily. Thus a person whose training is in law, engineering, or political science but who has done economic analysis for a number of years will probably be given a higher rating as an economist than a person who is professionally trained but who has had little experience. Once classified, he can build upon his experience and advance in grade.

Status and Working Conditions

The demand for economists has been brisk since 1950 and has probably exceeded the supply in all sectors, including federal service. In 1970 young economists could enter federal service at levels of GS-11 and GS-12 (earning from $11,233 to $13,389). Advancement is often rapid, and of course, the usual Civil Service fringe benefits relative to leave and retirement apply. These practical factors are by no means unattractive and compare favorably with those available to economists in business and academic life. Indeed, as the grade increases the pay scale soon overtakes most academic rates. A senior economist (GS-16), for example, with some years of experience can earn from $26,000 to $28,000. Few academic economists command base salaries of this level, although they may earn as much when all sources of income are considered. These are, of course, twelve-month salaries, while most academic base salaries are for nine months. Salaries in business are comparable, although once again those above $25,000 are infrequently encountered. The financial advantage may be offset by a feeling of being lost in the mass of federal employees, some inhibitions about publishing and speaking, and other areas in which the employee needs to conform to the federal personnel standards.[26]

Economic Advice and Analysis in the Executive Agencies

Although economists employed in the executive agencies are, by the nature of the tasks involved, more likely to be specialists and analysts than advisers, it is not unheard of for a secretary or agency head to have a formally designated economic adviser. For example, several economists served as economic advisers to Henry A. Wallace, the secretary of agriculture from 1932 to 1940. An economist in such a position must maintain a much broader outlook than his colleagues who deal with the specific issues which are the department's major tasks, for his function is to evaluate the impact of the department's policies upon the national economy and vice versa. In a large agency such as USDA his work often consists of coordinating data

---

[26] These problems are especially evident when security is paramount. The CIA, for example, employs economists, but their work is secret. An economist who leaves such an agency cannot cite his writings or say much about his work, which puts him at a disadvantage.

and drawing conclusions for the secretary. As a result, he has little opportunity to acquire a reputation. Furthermore, his connection with agency policy prohibits him from publishing anything even slightly controversial. Unless he has a strong academic background, his professional career and influence will probably be restricted to the agency or, at best, to other such agencies.

In the absence of a specific adviser, agencies depend on staff research groups. In this case, communication between adviser and advisee is generally by written memo rather than face-to-face discussion. The secretary may ask his adviser or assistants for a recommendation in order to help him formulate his views. In actual practice his request will probably involve various bureaus and divisions in which the actual economic analysis performed by numerous economists is passed along the line and pulled together at the top. Thus economic advice becomes a production line operation and is seldom concentrated in one man. While this process is very systematic and gives each part of the organization a chance to insert its views, it also presents the maximum opportunity for hedging and avoiding a strong position.

Although a surprising number of executive departments operated for years without making formal attempts to use economic analysis, several did recognize the economic implications of their work at an early date. It was completely understandable that many departments refused to concern themselves with economic matters. Any economic impact was remote: for example, the economic implications of the defense program in 1930 could be (and were) safely ignored.

The "old line" federal agencies—State, Agriculture, Commerce, and Labor—employ large numbers of economists. Fewer appear in departments such as Defense, but large numbers are employed in such newer departments as Housing and Urban Development. Independent organizations, including the Board of Governors of the Federal Reserve System, have always been large employers of economic talent. However, relatively small numbers appear in the legislative branch. While the overall tendency to employ economists in meaningful professional work is growing, it is still quite uneven among agencies and is recent in origin. The Council of Economic Advisers and the Joint Economic Committee, now the key economic groups in the federal establishment, are only twenty-five years old. Several agencies in the executive branch have made use of economic talent since the 1920s, although in relatively small numbers. Conversely, the Department of Agriculture has always hired many economists, especially agricultural economists.[27] The regulatory commissions, which one would expect to be major users of economists' services, have lagged behind. Apparently, their failure to keep abreast of the other agencies is due to low budgets and a generally legalistic philosophy which has often overshadowed the economic issues.

Regulatory Commissions and Economists

The Interstate Commerce Commission was outstanding among its peers in its early years and had a reputation for employing economists of high caliber. One cannot expect the ICC or any other agency to follow the academic practice of employing a large number of economists who engage in esoteric research. On one hand, the regulatory agency must deal with intensely pragmatic problems on a realistic schedule. On the other hand, it must engage in serious economic research and can fail to do so only at its peril. While it must meet day-to-day demands, the research arm of such an organization ideally should also engage in long-range studies which attempt to anticipate problems and forecast events. "Here-and-now" problems must, of course, receive priority. The economist whose forte is constructing elaborate but unrealistic models should not dominate the organization. In fact, the economist should not be in a policy-making position to the exclusion of others. Clair Wilcox has noted the dangers of the expert performing administrative tasks:

The expert is a specialist, highly skilled by training and experience within a narrow field. He is best used in a post where policy is prescribed and the scope of his discretion limited. His proper function is that of analyzing complex data and making individual determinations in accordance with settled principles. The members of a regulatory commis-

---

[27] Agricultural economists are a somewhat different breed. Although one of the most outstanding, the late John D. Black, was on the Harvard faculty, they are more frequently found in the land grant institutions where colleges of agriculture have long been important. In these institutions the agricultural economist is typically housed in the "ag" college while his conventional colleagues are found in business or arts and sciences. The two faculties often see little of each other. The USDA is, of course, the largest employer of these economists, both in Washington and in extension services. As enrollments in colleges of agriculture continue to decline, these economists increasingly turn to research (often USDA supported).

sion, on the other hand, are given broad discretion to define the public interest in the light of ambiguous statutory goals. Their task is largely that of formulating policy. In such a role, the expert is miscast. His special competence does not relate to definition of the public interest. His professionalism afflicts him with myopia. He views the problems of regulation through the blinders of his specialized techniques. Put him in command, and regulation will tend to be inflexible. It is important that experts be on a commission's staff. These specialists, of course, will not agree. The lawyers, the economists, and the engineers, within the limits of their disciplines, will offer varying advice. The commissioners themselves should be equipped to take a broader view. The expert, it has been said, should be on tap but not on top.[28]

In the final analysis, the economist in a regulatory agency must play the role of adviser, "devil's advocate," and forecaster of events. He must put the organization into its proper "environment." He is uniquely suited by training and temperament to this task.

An organization such as a regulatory commission has a vast responsibility to keep up with, or one hopes, to stay ahead of developments in the industry it regulates. It must be able to forecast changes and their impact. However, since appropriations have increased only moderately, it is likely that the many regulatory agencies have lacked the financial resources to upgrade and expand their research staffs. "Police type" agencies characteristically have a more difficult time with appropriations than such promotional "Santa Claus" types as Agriculture and Health, Education, and Welfare, which have clienteles to whom benefits accrue.

As we have noted, the demand for economists has been rising in both industry and academia. The advantages of federal employment, which were potent in pre-World War II days, have lost some force; and though economists entering federal service have increased in absolute numbers, other opportunities open to them have greatly expanded. Furthermore, in recent years "the action" for those who want government careers has been not in regulatory agencies, which were pioneering in 1910 and 1935, but in the Council of Economic Advisers, the poverty program, and other groups dealing with "hot" issues. Consequently, older federal establishments have had to fight

---

[28] Reprinted with permission from Clair Wilcox, *Public Policies Toward Business* (Homewood, Ill.: Richard D. Irwin, 1960), p. 763.

harder to attract outstanding staff members. Regulatory commissions, at least on the surface, do not appear to be dramatic. Compared to the CEA, for example, they are seldom in the mainstream of events. Young economists are naturally anxious to enter growing and vigorous agencies where they can help form current policy and encounter considerable interchange between economists in the agency and those in universities. Again, the CEA is outstanding, as are the Board of Governors of the Federal Reserve System and the staff of the Joint Economic Committee. Well-qualified economists can shift from academic life to Washington and back again to the campus, a very attractive feature. Regulatory bodies offer few such opportunities. These factors interact and reinforce each other. Bright young men follow other bright young men. As a result, it is doubtful that the regulatory commissions have been in the mainstream for several decades.[29]

The organization of regulatory commissions has not made for a happy research climate. Throughout its life, and especially in recent years, the Interstate Commerce Commission, to cite a typical example, has had to cope with a constantly increasing work load and a reluctance on the part of Congress to increase its funds. The major problem of the commission, as is true of all such bodies, is to allocate time for the many duties which need daily attention and at the same time to provide for high-level policy making. The commission's policy has not been marked by sound organization and frequently lacks structure. In fact, one author has indicated that the Interstate Commerce Commission does not make policy and merely puts forth a mass of small decisions on minor points.[30]

There is much merit in this view. Many articles and academic theses have been written on various facets of commission policy, but tracing this policy on a comprehensive basis is indeed a difficult task.

[29] It is more than coincidence that many economists who have made a name for themselves in studying regulatory bodies are past middle age and that few replacements are on the horizon. See, for example, the list of doctoral dissertation subjects published each fall in the *American Economic Review*. Few are in the area of regulation.

[30] See D. S. Watson, *Economic Policy: Business and Government* (Boston: Houghton Mifflin Co., 1960), p. 398. See also Marver H. Bernstein, *Regulating Business by Independent Regulatory Commission* (Princeton: Princeton University Press, 1955).

Clearly, the central problem is not the technical mode of organization but the philosophy with which the group undertakes its work.[31]

It appears that the work of the economist in regulatory agencies can be carried out on two levels. On the upper level, an economist would engage in long-range research, attempting to predict the direction of competition and changes among the modes and their market shares. This sort of information is vital to the efficient administration of a regulatory program. Economists on this level might even question the concept of the public utility per se. On a lower level, the services of the economist would be useful in such matters as measuring the impact of potential entrants into industry, rate questions, and other essentially microeconomic problems. Some of these matters are, of course, subject to inquiry by the Department of Transportation and other federal agencies (for instance, Defense and Agriculture) which have collateral interests, but the ICC still retains the basic responsibility for administering the regulatory program.[32] Most regulatory agencies are in the same general situation, and some— notably the Federal Trade Commission—are under increasingly heavy fire by critics.

Economists "On the Hill"

Except for its use of the Joint Economic Committee and the Joint Committee on Internal Revenue Taxation, the legislative branch has in the past depended on economists only for special studies (for example, the famous Temporary National Economic Committee in the late 1930s). However, in recent decades several standing committees have acquired full-time professional economists. Monopoly and antitrust have been of continuous concern to the Congress, and the committees dealing with these problems have almost always employed a half-dozen or so economists. A recent issue of the *Congressional Directory* indicates that one or more professional staff

[31] Despite the increasing work load, personnel is a constant problem. For example, in the fiscal 1967 budget, forty-five ICC jobs were eliminated from the request as compared to the 1966 budget. Although the total request rose from $27.5 million to $27.7 million, personnel was reduced from 2,463 to 2,418.

[32] Some of these agencies (often with more research money than the ICC), carry on elaborate programs. The USDA, for example, makes in-depth studies on transportation of farm products, rate questions, etc., which might more properly be carried on by the commission itself.

members with the title of economist are employed by each of three Senate and joint committees—Senate Agriculture, Joint Economic, and Internal Revenue Taxation.[33]

However, many committees list under professional staff "consultants" or "specialists," individuals who are, if not so designated, clearly economists by the nature of their tasks. The Library of Congress, a legislative institution, employs economists as well as experts on such fields as political science and constitutional law in its Legislative Reference Service, a body designed to serve the research needs of the Congress.

The LRS section of the *Congressional Directory* lists a number of economists under several special categories—for example, agriculture, Soviet economics, and transportation. A reasonable estimate would place between fifty and seventy-five professional economists "on the Hill."[34] No data exist about the number of congressmen who seek economic advice directly from professionals on the various staffs or from outside.

Senators and representatives traditionally have been pragmatic and have shown little inclination to seek out expert advice, except perhaps on highly technical subjects such as atomic energy. However, increasing evidence suggests that the younger, more highly educated legislators are more apt to be aware of the complexity of socioeconomic issues and value professional counsel.[35]

Where the Action Is

The influential economists in government center in a few organizations—the Council of Economic Advisers, the Treasury, the Board of Governors of the Federal Reserve System, and the White House staff; and on the legislative side, the Joint Committee on Internal Revenue Taxation, the Joint Economic Committee, and the Antimonopoly Subcommittee. These twenty or thirty economists are in

[33] U.S., Congress, *Congressional Directory*, 91st Cong. (Washington, D.C.: Government Printing Office, March, 1969).

[34] See John M. Blair, "Lawyers and Economists in Antitrust: A Marriage of Necessity If Not Convenience," *Proceedings*, American Bar Association, Vols. 20–23, 1962–63 (April, 1962), pp. 29–37.

[35] Only on rare occasions does a professional economist reach high elective office. Former Senator Paul H. Douglas of the University of Chicago is the only recent example. Elected in 1948, he served until his defeat in 1966 by Senator Charles H. Percy.

key spots. Service on this level is exciting and rewarding to the profession. These economists are quite often the most capable the profession has to offer, and those on the CEA especially are leading members of the profession. As we have noted, many high-level economists are at home both in government service and academic life and often shift back and forth.

The federal establishment is a large and complex organization employing more than 2.5 million people (1.9 million of them white collar workers). Professional economists make up only a minute fraction by even the most generous definition. Of these, a mere handful are in truly influential positions. In *The Role of the Economist in Government Policy Making,* I made an effort to identify the influential economists by seeking the opinions of their peers.[36] In the final analysis, it was estimated that about one hundred economists had occupied influential posts since 1920. These men were found in a relatively few parts of the establishment—the Council of Economic Advisers, the Treasury, the Federal Reserve, the Bureau of the Budget, the Department of Commerce, and a few isolated in the legislative branch in places such as the Joint Committee on Internal Revenue Taxation. It is both surprising and disappointing to find so few in the regulatory agencies, where one would expect to find them playing key roles.

The Seat of Power: Economists at the White House

Since the passage of the Employment Act of 1946, the Council of Economic Advisers has been *the* formal channel for providing the president with economic advice. Before and to a degree since that time the president has often utilized other, more informal sources. There are, of course, numerous sources of economic advice available to the president if he wishes to use them, but it seems unlikely that he would have ready access to professional economists outside the executive office of the president. The president's time and energy are two of the most scarce items in Washington. Various accounts written about the Council of Economic Advisers make it clear that even the council chairman has occasional difficulty in bringing matters directly before the president.[37]

Considerable competition for the president's ear is natural. As a

[36] See especially Chapters 2 and 3.
[37] See, for example, Nourse, *Economics in the Public Service.*

result, numerous economic advisers (often, no doubt, self-appointed) have been in or close to the White House since 1920. However, few of those who have functioned in this area have been professional economists in the modern sense of the word.

Under the Employment Act of 1946, the president has a clear obligation to entertain proposals and advice from the council (although he can do so in a minimal fashion, as Truman did with Nourse), but his relationship with other economists both within and outside the government is entirely what he chooses to make it.[38] None of the five presidents who have served since the council was established have ignored the council, though they might, in effect, do so if they wished. Before 1932, no economist had been on the White House staff, although a few had served the president upon request. For instance, Julius Klein served as adviser to Hoover, although formally he was in the Commerce Department. FDR was apt to seek advice from many sources, but by his second term his once close relationship with the brain trust economists had changed. While some economists continued to be influential in various departments, their direct contact with the president was progressively less and by the beginning of the Second World War seems to have ceased entirely. Early in the Second World War, FDR did, however, appoint a full-time economic adviser borrowed from the Federal Reserve Board. This man was Lauchlin Currie (holder of a Harvard Ph.D.), who had been a New Deal figure and an adjunct member of the brain trust for some time. Currie served as assistant director of research for the Federal Reserve Board of Governors but later left government service.[39]

By Truman's time, the White House staff had grown substantially from the informal one of Coolidge and even in comparison to that of Roosevelt. It had become common to have advisers—science advisers, military advisers, and advisers on problems of minority groups, to name but a few. These men often worked on a full-time basis, and unlike Roosevelt's days, they had more formal titles and fairly well-defined responsibilities. Truman was a better and more systematic

[38] In a letter, Nourse told the author, "[Truman] never bothered what my views were" (Nourse to Norton, 23 December 1969).

[39] Currie was, in 1970, a professor of economics at Simon Fraser University and an active writer. In his White House job Currie, like many of Roosevelt's aides, was frustrated because of the undefined nature of his duties. See Herbert Stein, *The Fiscal Revolution in America* (Chicago: University of Chicago Graduate School of Business, 1969).

administrator than FDR, but he was highly pragmatic. He had less
inclination toward consulting advisers in general and had little use
for economists. When the Employment Act of 1946 was passed, Mr.
Truman made use of the Council of Economic Advisers, although it
is unlikely that he fully understood it. Many economists felt that
Truman failed to use the council as it was intended. The Congress
became somewhat restive, and in 1952 the council might very well
have been allowed to pass from the scene had it not been for Eisenhower's intervention and some fast parliamentary footwork in the
Congress.

Eisenhower and the Resident Economist

Despite the fact that the council has formal responsibility for advising the president on economic matters, it is obvious that the president may wish to have a personal adviser or someone who can in-
terpret the advice rendered by the council and handle the various
economic matters coming to the White House for solution. Eisenhower, a devotee of the staff system, adopted such a personal adviser.

Sherman Adams has traced the way in which Eisenhower acquired
his staff economist, Gabriel Hauge:

I found Hauge at the Eisenhower headquarters at Denver when I arrived in August, 1952 to take over my staff duties. He came to Eisenhower on the recommendation of the Dewey organization where he had
worked under Elliot Bell of the McGraw-Hill Publishing Company.
Hauge was one of the ablest men Dewey had. Previously he had taught
economics at Harvard and Princeton and had directed statistical research
for the New York State Banking Department. On the Eisenhower campaign train in 1952, Hauge labored with Robert Cutler in what we called
a little facetiously "the speech-rescue squad," preparing notes for Eisenhower's whistle stop talks and revising the final drafts of major speeches.
I learned then that Hauge's outstanding quality was versatility; along
with his fine grasp of economics as it applied to public affairs—he under-
stands, for example, the Federal Reserve System, something that not too
many people comprehend—he could write about and discuss almost anything in the wide field of federal government responsibilities with an
unusual command of the language. Eisenhower was impressed by Hauge,
too, but after the election I had some difficulty persuading him to add
Hauge to our staff. Eisenhower thought of Hauge primarily as an economist and he was not sure that he needed a personal adviser in the

White House. . . . Fortunately, Eisenhower was won over in favor of Hauge because he decided that this particular economist could also be useful as a writer and a general adviser, which indeed he was.[40]

Hauge later participated in the choice of Arthur F. Burns as chairman of the council and lent his support to efforts to instruct the president on various economic matters (and upon occasion, no doubt, to overcome the authority and prestige of the late George M. Humphrey).[41]

Aside from giving or interpreting advice, the main duty of the White House economist is what the late Gerhard Colm called the "fire brigade function."[42] That is, he fields the various economic issues landing on the president's desk that the council is too busy to look after or that have a strong political orientation. Further, the staff economist can often function, as Hauge did, as a general staff adviser on a wide range of economic and related issues. Many economists with White House staff assignments have not borne the title of economic adviser but have actually served in this capacity. Their statuses apparently have been more in the nature of general staff than as advisers in the Hauge manner or in semispecialists roles such as agricultural economists.

Relatively few economists are qualified for such a post, for the job requires a combination of personal and professional qualities that are not often encountered. In addition to his professional skills, the White House economist must be willing to operate in a political atmosphere in which his advice may be overbalanced by political considerations or perhaps ignored entirely. He must be willing to subordinate himself to the president's program and to work in harmony with the rest of the White House staff and the administration team. Clearly, he must also have a flair for translating economic concepts into lay terms. It frequently has been reported that President Kennedy enjoyed economic discourse and had some interest in methodology.[43] He was the exception. Taking the time limitation into

[40] *First Hand Report* (New York: Harper & Row, Publishers, Incorporated, 1961), p. 55.

[41] *Ibid.*, pp. 361, 386.

[42] U.S. Congress, Joint Economic Committee, "Twentieth Anniversary of the Employment Act of 1946," *An Economic Symposium*, 89th Cong., 2nd sess. (Washington, D.C.: Government Printing Office, 1966), p. 81.

[43] See Canterbery, *Economics on a New Frontier*, pp. 9, 13; and Theodore C. Sorensen, *Kennedy* (New York: Harper and Row, Bantam Ed., 1966).

account, no other president is on record as having an interest in how the results were obtained. The president must, by necessity, be highly pragmatic in his approach to matters. The White House staff member is presented with a problem which in most cases requires an answer as soon as possible. Within a few hours or days, he may see the president again to give him the answer or at least to recommend a course of action. What the president needs least is a long, complex analysis of the variable factors which had to be considered in order to arrive at a conclusion.

As we have seen, Eisenhower adopted the practice of using a staff economist. Walter Heller, Kennedy's CEA chairman, apparently believed that the council could work more efficiently without someone in this capacity on the White House staff. Gerhard Colm argued that this feeling was probably wrong since, as a consequence, the CEA staff would be spread thin and burdened with the political-economic matters which crop up in the White House and must be dealt with at that level.

It is apparent that while the White House resident economist might be useful in many ways (even as a general utility man), he might also be a major source of administration conflict. If he interposes himself between the CEA and the president or "interprets" the CEA's advice, a major problem may arise. In fact, the economic adviser attached to the White House staff is in direct competition with the council. By his location he is apt to see more of the president and to develop a better personal rapport with him than the chairman of the council can. Of course, some danger of functional overlap always exists because someone on the White House staff coordinates affairs in regard to such areas as defense, transportation, and conservation and may thus conflict with the cabinet officials responsible for those areas. Another potential problem stems from the fact that one more voice is added to those already concerned with economic policy. In any major economic policy matter, the president presumably would wish to consult the secretary of the Treasury, the chairman of the Federal Reserve Board of Governors, the director of the Bureau of the Budget, and perhaps others in addition to the council. Thus the White House adviser might merely represent another level to be dealt with in policy clearance.

The confusion might be compounded by the fact that "White House staff" and "presidential adviser" or "presidential assistant" are very elastic terms indeed, and to the outsider, they are quite impressive. Consequently, an economist on the White House staff might, if he chose, vastly overstate his influence and prestige. Also, in the game of palace politics an individual who wished to do so might undercut the council. The chairman of the council has a more or less structured job, whereas a "presidential adviser" might be in a position to "wheel and deal."

How They Got There

Although presidents are apt to be acquainted with businessmen, they are not likely to have widespread acquaintances with professional economists, especially those in academic life. Eisenhower had never heard of Arthur Burns, even though he had been professor of economics at Columbia when Eisenhower was its president.

Kennedy, on the other hand, had no staff economic adviser but had many academic contacts and was a tireless questioner of economists who crossed his path. Both Schlesinger and Sorensen note instances when he sought answers from such professionals as Paul Samuelson, Robert Nathan, and Seymour Harris (then a Harvard professor). Sorensen notes that "the President paid most attention to Heller and Dillon but he also mixed in his own readings, observations and sense of the national congressional mood."[44] Kennedy asked Paul Samuelson to head up an antirecession task force prior to his election, and according to Sorensen, this group had a major impact on policy. It also "redoubled Kennedy's futile efforts to induce Samuelson to leave the academic calm that he relished and join the new frontier."[45] Other economists who came to attention through service on task forces were John Kenneth Galbraith, Carl Keysen, James Tobin, and Walter Heller (the latter two later joined the CEA).

One of the pitfalls of such service was illustrated by W. W. Rostow (an economic historian), who left the faculty of the Massachusetts Institute of Technology to join the Kennedy staff. Rostow stayed on under Johnson and became a somewhat controversial figure, apparently because of his views on the Vietnam war. At any rate, Rostow decided not to return to MIT and accepted an invitation to join

[44] *Kennedy*, p. 443.
[45] *Ibid.*, p. 267.

the faculty of the University of Texas at the close of the Johnson administration.

The routes to advisership are diverse. FDR and JFK both appointed their former professors or persons recommended by them. Leon Keyserling (the second CEA chairman) came to the Truman council on the recommendation of the late Senator Robert F. Wagner of New York, and Eisenhower's Hauge had performed well in the Dewey campaign. Walter Heller met Kennedy almost by accident. After the first Kennedy-Nixon television debate, the candidate visited Minneapolis. Heller was tired and decided not to attend a dinner in JFK's honor, but on a whim he went to the hotel later hoping to be able to advise Kennedy to hit the recession issue harder. En route to Kennedy's room, he met Hubert Humphrey, an old acquaintance, who introduced him. After a discussion on economic issues, Heller quickly became a Kennedy convert, and in mid-December he was offered and accepted the CEA chairmanship.[46]

Informal advisers appear to have an instinct for survival; some have served both Republican and Democratic presidents. Robert Nathan, the late Walter Stewart, Leon Keyserling (CEA chairman under Truman), and others have been or were advisers for many years. Most drift into or out of White House circles, depending on political fortunes.[47] Because the CEA is made up almost exclusively of academic economists, it recruits by personal contacts in academic institutions. Also, the council has no doubt had a hand in choosing people for the general advisory process. Its own professional standards have been high, and it is likely that most presidents choose a personal adviser with the CEA in mind. However, a president might also want someone who has the prestige and authority to counterbalance the CEA in order to obtain a broader range of advice.

Insiders and Outsiders

The president's advisory resources have been greatly enhanced by the establishment of the CEA and the more frequent use of staff

[46] Lester Tanzer, ed., *The Kennedy Circle* (Washington, D.C.: Luce, 1961), pp. 98–99.
[47] Nathan, for example, advised FDR, Truman, and JFK and served as adviser to Humphrey in the 1968 campaign. His firm, Robert Nathan Associates, has close labor union ties. Likewise, Keyserling has close labor and liberal ties and is a lawyer-consulting economist in Washington.

experts. However, he may still wish to seek advice outside the formal structure. Outsiders play a much different role than those who are formally attached to the executive office. These advisers are often unknown, or at least the extent of their influence is generally not known. They advise the president "after hours," at dinners, on the golf course, or in other informal ways. Having no formal responsibility and no direct subordinate relationship to the president, they may be able to render more useful advice than those who are within the formal structure. They may or may not have a personal ax to grind. All presidents have used such sources of advice, and since these relationships are confidential, it is difficult to trace their effectiveness.

Obviously, Hoover asked for comments and advice from the business leaders with whom he conferred. Can one doubt that Eisenhower received advice from the guests (mostly business leaders) at his famous stag dinners, or that Kennedy found his contacts with labor leaders and other White House visitors (whom he routinely questioned) useful? Unfortunately, of course, the outsider may present something of a problem since he can afford to ignore the implications of his advice or may exploit his relationship with the president for reasons of personal publicity or advantage. It is probable that most outside advisers have been less influential than the press reports devoted to them would seem to indicate. This is especially true of "general advisers," the elder statesman type who may offer experience but who can hardly be informed on all specific issues. These men are often self-appointed, to the despair of the formal staff.

The outsider faces another disadvantage, for he may not be in possession of all the facts and is forced to take a narrower view than the insiders who are on the day-to-day scene of action. When the formal machinery was modest or nonexistent, the outsider probably played a much more significant part than has been the case in recent years.

The president must, of course, be aware of the advantages and disadvantages of both insiders and outsiders and, one would hope, of the strong points, weak points, blind spots, and biases of his advisers. His task is to blend their advice, carefully sorting out the good from the bad. Undoubtedly, much of the advice tendered, especially when it is unasked for, is ignored. The president listens politely, makes a noncommittal observation, and forgets the whole thing. One is reminded, for instance, that a well-known presidential adviser is reported to have told JFK that the major problems of his term would be national security and control of inflation.

The Economist and the Nature of the Advisory Function

For many reasons the economist may be reluctant to play the role of an anonymous adviser required of one who serves the government or the business firm on a high level. If he accepts such service he must resign himself to the fact that his advice may (though scientifically sound) be ignored or distorted for practical or political purposes. He may find that he is unable to defend his professional integrity. He must be ready to see his carefully crafted gems of analysis brushed aside by those who have neither knowledge of nor appreciation for his science. Most serious of all, the adviser must be able to separate and compartmentalize his technical, analytical skill and his value judgments. For most economists and other professionals, this is a difficult task.

The work of the adviser proceeds on two levels. On the first level, he supplies economic information to his superior. This task is essentially one of technical analysis, and the role of the economist ends when he has made the facts known to his superior, a line official who must then act on the basis of the economist's advice and other available data and advice.

On the second level, the economist goes a step further and using the facts, *advises* his superior on a course of action. On the first level, technical skill is a requirement. On the second, judgment, maturity, and personal rapport between adviser and client are also required. In short, high-level advice is as much an art form as a scientific exercise. Most well-trained economists can operate successfully on the first level. Competence on the second is more rarely found. The true high-level adviser generally functions in such a way that it is difficult to draw a line between economic advice per se and generalized advice. Just as a mature and wise legal counselor transcends the merely legal and becomes a trusted general adviser, the high-level economic adviser may go beyond the technical level of economic advice.

By their very nature, economists and executives are apt to differ. Economists, especially those based in academia, traditionally have been trained to be observers, not participants. Many economists' scientific sense cautions them against projecting personal views into the situation. A man who reaches high government office or the presidency of a large firm is, by contrast, a man of action and decision who is apt to be impatient with fine technical distinctions and will have little time for methodology. The economist may find it difficult to work for such a man on a daily basis. Perhaps this problem is not as serious as it seems since a fair number of economists have successfully moved into managerial jobs, a fact which would have seemed very unlikely a generation ago.

The well-trained economist is skilled in the manipulation of data and concepts and is able to perform such technical tasks as national income analysis and the translation of data on consumption and other functions into reasonably accurate forecasts. All these skills are necessary, but they must be supplemented by personal qualities.

Economists are frequently apt to seek complex solutions at the expense of immediate, practical matters. Though this tendency is acceptable in academic life, it is not satisfactory in the forum or the market place. Thus many of the qualities which have served the economist as academician stand for little in the world of Pennsylvania Avenue or in the executive suite, where he has recently arrived to ply his trade.

Professional Problems

The most frequent problem facing the federal economist is one common to many professionals in government—frustration arising from the inescapable fact that decisions at high levels are often made by politicians for political reasons. Economists who have formulated sound economic reasons for a course of action may be very unhappy to see their conclusions ignored for the sake of political reality. This is a frequent problem in the regulatory agencies and seems to be reflected in their work, as we have seen.

Another problem which some economists in government face is that they feel they have a mission to change the world in their own image. Some economists close to the levers of power suffer from this ailment, which was often attributed to those in the high levels during the New Deal and to others more recently. On the other hand, some have followed the traditional approach and have been too reluctant to interfere. Gardner Ackley, a former CEA chairman, seems to strike a modern and workable position when he observes:

Frankly, I believe that these often discussed problems are largely false problems. As an economic advisor, I do not feel that I should hesitate to express my views on questions of this sort. Those in authority get plenty of advice from others who show no great delicacy in distinguishing technical questions within their competence from questions of values. The President hears from other members of his Administration, from businessmen, from labor leaders, from journalists—yes, from economists. If his economic advisor refrains from advice on the gut questions of policy, the President should and will get another one.

Moreover, in practice, most attempted distinctions between questions of technical economics and problems of values break down on examination. Price stability, for example—even full employment—is surely not an ultimate value. Price stability is a desirable and urgent goal of public policy primarily because its absence creates economic dislocations and strains. There is an element of truth in the view that attempts to increase employment in a given year at the cost of inflation really mean that policies will be necessary later on that will reduce employment in some future year.[48]

Young economists seem to be leaning toward the Ackley view and are less apt to stand aside.

Advisers, especially those on the president's staff or in the CEA, face serious problems regarding the disclosure of exchanges between themselves and the president. As the first CEA chairman, Edwin G. Nourse took a stand against testifying before the Congress. Arthur Burns, who testified on occasion, was careful to avoid issues which were under current discussion. Leon Keyserling, on the other hand, had no hesitation about being an advocate.

Nourse's view was clearly that of a person who thought of himself as a *confidential adviser to the president.* He did not see himself as an active participant in the president's program, involved in day-to-day affairs or in the promotion of the program. In his view, the council was to operate in a detached fashion by giving the president technical advice.

Nourse's fellow CEA members Leon Keyserling, and to a lesser extent, John D. Clark, did not embrace his view and soon made it clear that they did not see anything improper in the council's active participation in the president's program. Keyserling also was not op-

[48] "Contribution of Economists to Policy Formulation," p. 176.

posed to testifying before Congress, as was Nourse. Keyserling stated his philosophy thus:

It is clear that the members of the Council are employees of and advisers to the President, and that they are not employees of and advisers to the Congress in the same sense. But this does not mean, in my opinion, that the members of the Council cannot or should not testify before, cooperate and consult with, and in a sense give advice to, committees of the Congress just as this is done by heads of other agencies in the executive branch, and even other agencies in the Executive Office of the President such as the National Security Board, who are appointed by the President and confirmed by the Senate under statutes defining their functions and responsibilities and who are employees of the advisers to the President in the sense that they work under his direction as members of his "official family" and may, of course, be dismissed by him. . . .

In appearing before committees of Congress in this role, I cannot see where the Council of Economic Advisers is doing any different or appearing in any different light from what is done by heads of other agencies working in different fields. . . .[49]

Burns's operating philosophy was noticeably different from Keyserling's. In fact, he indicated a desire to play a role more in the Nourse tradition. The issue of his relationship to the Congress arose at the time of his confirmation. At that time he told Senator John Sparkman, "My own personal inclination would be to stay out of the limelight, make my recommendation to the President, indicate to him what the basis of the recommendation is,—and then having done that, to remain eternally quiet."[50] Although Burns did not take as extreme a position as Nourse did, he apparently agreed that his usefulness would be diminished if he responded to all questions from a political group. In Burns's view, there were several areas in which he could cooperate without impairing his advisory relationship to the president. He recognized that council members were more than

---

[49] U.S., Congress, Subcommittee on General Credit Control and Debt Management, *Monetary Policy and the Public Debt Hearings*, 82nd Cong. (Washington, D.C.: Government Printing Office, March, 1952).

[50] U.S., Congress, Senate Committee on Banking and Currency, Hearings on the Confirmation of Arthur F. Burns as Chairman of the Council of Economic Advisers, 83rd Cong., 1st sess. Quoted in Corrine Silverman, *The President's Council of Economic Advisers*, Inter-University Case Program, No. 48 (Indianapolis: Bobbs-Merrill Co., 1959), p. 16.

advisers; they were also "administrators" of the Employment Act of 1946. Thus it would be proper for council members to advise Congress in this regard. A second area in which Burns was willing to testify was with reference to a technical matter such as the derivation of data. Also, he was quite willing, of course, to testify on matters relating to the council per se, such as defending its budget requests.[51] Concerning a fourth area, testimony dealing with economic conditions and policy, Burns notes two major dangers in testifying:

First, in some cases the President had to adopt policies that he didn't like and that I didn't like. He had to do it for reasons of overall political policy, but his heart was bleeding over it. What should I do before a committee of Congress in such a case? Should I criticize the President when I happen to know that he shares my views? Would that be fair? On the other hand, how could I say to a congressional committee that something is sound when I believed otherwise?

The other major danger in testifying is that once an adviser takes a strong position in public, he is apt to become a prisoner of that position. I wanted to give the President the fullest benefit of my knowledge and thought. Hence I wanted to be free to advise the President one way one day, and yet be able if necessary to go in the next day and say, "I've been thinking it over. What I told you yesterday was wrong. I overlooked some important points. What really ought to be done is thus and so."[52]

Burns notes that in his view, both Keyserling and Nourse took extreme positions, but he admits that Nourse made it possible for him to do his job. This issue of advocacy versus objectivity and a confidential relationship with the president is far from solved.

Economists at the lower levels do not, of course, face such severe problems, but they may feel equal frustration because they are so far down the ladder that what professional ideas they have are of little value or consequence. At the very highest levels, one finds great excitement and professional satisfaction. At lower levels, matters are more routine; and the Civil Service is not an ideal career for everyone. However, economists have made great strides in government since 1930, and they perform an increasingly essential service.

[51] Nourse agrees with these points saying, "I only wish I had been smart enough to differentiate these cases as explicitly as Burns has done from the fourth issue, the one on which I took my stand." See Silverman, *The President's Economic Advisers*, p. 16.

[52] *Ibid.*, p. 17.

The ultimate contribution by economists to the governmental process is difficult to measure. Considered as useless or worse in the 1930s, by the 1960s they were held in high regard by the more influential persons in government and enjoyed a "good press." It is interesting to note that although they had arrived on the governmental scene earlier in Britain than in the United States, their stature in Britain had by the late 1960s diminished somewhat.[53] Whether anyone could have cured Britain's chronic economic difficulties is, of course, open to question.

[53] See T. W. Hutchinson, *Economics and Economic Policy in Britain, 1946–66* (London: Allen and Unwin, 1968); and Alec Carincross, "Economists in Government," *Lloyds Bank Review*, No. 95 (January, 1970), pp. 1–18. Likewise, U.S. economists were being subjected to critical comment. See "Worldly Prophets," *New York Times*, 27 December 1970, Sec. 3, p. 1; and Robert Lekachman, "The Quarrelsome Economists," *New Leader*, 13 October 1969, p. 9ff. A good discussion of the problems between economists and the media is found in "Economists Consider Economic Reporters and Vice Versa" (a panel discussion), *Proceedings*, American Economic Association, Vol. LXII, No. 2 (May, 1972).

5

The Professional Economist in the Business World

THE alliance between the businessman and the economist was not formed quickly or easily.[1] Several factors in addition to the economists' reluctance to leave the classroom
seem responsible for the delays. First, the business community looked
upon practical training with favor and viewed academic training
with some suspicion before 1900 and in some cases much later. Staff
experts, now much in evidence, were not widely used before 1920,
and entry into the higher levels of the business world was more apt
to be through experience than via formal education. Second, the
rising prominence of economists in the New Deal years did not en-
hance their position in the eyes of the business community and delayed their acceptance for another decade. Let us examine these
factors in greater detail.

Formal Education and Business Before 1920

We have seen that economists were not inclined to involve themselves deeply in the nonacademic world before 1920. Let us turn now
to the major force which delayed the entry of economists into the
business world, namely, the general attitude of business toward
formal education in the years before 1920.[2] The businessman of this

[1] A major portion of this chapter appeared originally as *The Professional
Economist: His Role in Government and Industry*, Volume 19 in the Essays
in Economic Series, Bureau of Business and Economic Research, College of
Business Administration, University of South Carolina, Columbia, South Carolina, 1969.
[2] See Robert A. Gordon and James E. Howell, *Higher Education for Business*
(New York: Columbia University Press, 1959).

era was far from convinced of the merits of formal education as a requirement for business success.

Of the financial and industrial giants active before 1900, only a handful had received much formal education beyond the high school level, and many had not gone that far. Although business leaders at the very top tended to be more highly educated than is often supposed (especially those in finance, who were sometimes educated abroad), those in the middle management ranks rarely had received much formal education.[3]

Also, the higher education available during this era was oriented toward the liberal arts. J. P. Morgan, for example, was trained in both the United States and Germany in mathematics, a common academic background for financiers at the time.[4] The vast numbers now going from collegiate schools of business into industry were nonexistent. People usually entered business through the ranks in the "Horatio Alger" tradition. In some cases, commercial education was a means of entry; or in railroading, for example, engineering was a popular route. But generally a man entered the firm at the clerical level and took his chances on learning as he advanced. Collegiate business schools were in operation by the turn of the century (Wharton in 1884 and Harvard Graduate School of Business in 1908), but they were established to deal with such applied problems as accounting and railroad management. Many years were to pass before they reached their present status.[5]

After 1920 undergraduate schools of business became much more common, but the economist as such was still looked upon as superfluous to the business team. He was viewed as a fellow who "built boats in the basement," harmless but of no practical value in solving hardheaded problems, a theoretician who offered certain required courses to be passed and forgotten as soon as possible.

[3] See, for example, Thomas C. Cochran, *Railroad Leaders, 1845–1890* (Cambridge, Mass.: Harvard University Press, 1953).

[4] Morgan was a second generation businessman who had been given the benefits of an established position. Most of his contemporaries came up through the ranks.

[5] Even in these institutions economics was regarded as a subject for the economists, although it was taught to the students. The economists and M.B.A. faculty members held different viewpoints, and while these differences have not entirely disappeared, they have narrowed considerably. The M.B.A. was regarded as the professional degree in business while the M.A. or Ph.D. were the goals of those aspiring to acadmic employment.

For the most part, business schools concentrated on the applied aspects of business training and until recent years did not focus on the business firm in the context of society as a whole. This attitude generally suited the business community, whose members often looked upon the "B" schools as suppliers of middle management talent but seldom as sources of new ideas.

The businessman not only looked to the ranks for potential executive talent; but he also was much less inclined to use staff specialists than is now the practice. Specialists now on corporate staffs tending to such matters as industrial relations, community relations, or advertising, to name a few, would have been unheard of in 1890 and encountered only in the most progressive firms even by the late 1920s.[6] By the 1970s, of course, firms had come under great pressure to consider ecology, minority opportunities, and other issues which would have never occurred to the businessman of 1920 in his wildest dreams. When governmental influence was at a minimum and the business world was relatively uncomplicated, this view was, of course, entirely rational. Much of what the modern business economist does would have been unnecessary in 1900 or 1920, even assuming that the required data were available.

Let us now explore the second factor which delayed the formation of an alliance between the economist and the businessman, namely, the New Deal. As we have seen, the New Deal brought the economist out of his ivory tower and into the forum; but as he rose to prominence in the federal establishment, his prestige declined in the business community.

The Economist and the New Deal

As we saw in Chapter 4, Roosevelt enlisted the aid of various academic economists in his efforts to define issues and discover new ideas. These advisers, collectively known in newspaper parlance as the "brain trust," became conspicuous figures in the early New Deal years.

Their influence, although likely overrated, was widely discussed. Whatever their positive accomplishments in Washington, their prominence in the New Deal acted to broaden the gulf between economists and the business community. Many became the prime targets of anti–

---

[6] Henry Ford was perhaps the last figure in a major business to operate in an informal manner—no titles, no staff specialists, etc. Most sources make it clear that he felt even lawyers were excess baggage.

New Deal businessmen, and the acceptance of economists into business was further delayed.

Growing Involvement in Peace and War

As the years passed, however, many factors conducive to an alliance between economists and businessmen began to be felt. The major factor at work outside the profession was the increasingly complex business-government relationship. This involvement, which grew in scope from the early 1930s on, made it necessary for the businessman to pay some attention to the atmosphere in which the firm operated. The trend was first evident in such traditionally regulated industries as transportation and public utilities. As the 1930s progressed into the war years, the area of federal influence gradually expanded to cover the whole range of industry. The war, in particular, made it necessary for the firm to have a good picture of the industry as a whole and greatly stimulated the gathering and analysis of economic data.

More progressive firms began to recognize the value of staff specialists of all types as business problems became more complex. Concurrently, businessmen became accustomed to and grew less hostile toward those entering the firm through formal education. Economic data, the economist's raw material, began to be accumulated, and he was able to perform his functions more efficiently as a result. These changes were brought to a head by the Second World War, and the "new economist" began to emerge.

The Second World War speeded this process because economists had an opportunity to demonstrate their expertise.[7] Problems of materials, shortages, price control, allocation of goods, and other matters were more concrete than their depression counterparts and thus lent themselves to analysis, especially by the neoclassical economists whose tool kit was appropriate for these tasks.

Many economists served capably during the war in such hard-headed agencies as the Office of Strategic Services, the War Production Board, the Board of Economic Warfare, and the Office of Price Administration; and after the war in the Agency for International

---

[7] John Kenneth Galbraith notes that much of the economists' growing acceptability stems from such service in World War II federal agencies. See Galbraith, *American Capitalism: The Concept of Countervailing Power* (Boston: Houghton Mifflin Co., 1952).

Development, the Central Intelligence Agency, and the Korean War agencies. The role of the academic economists was especially important in the war agencies since a fair number of them remained in federal service or returned at frequent intervals. Theodore White notes that Edward S. Mason, a Harvard professor who served as chief economist in the Office of Strategic Services, brought to Washington several young economists who later served in key positions.[8]

For several reasons, this wartime era is more important than it appears at first glance. In the first place, young academic economists with high professional training became acquainted with equally trained businessmen. It is unlikely that they would have become acquainted under normal circumstances. Secondly, these men were given an unusual opportunity to demonstrate their abilities under fluid conditions. In wartime the government was able to tap resources of talent and information in the United States and abroad which otherwise would have been unavailable. In addition, federal employees were able to operate on a level and to encompass a scope of operations which would have been impossible in peacetime; and as a consequence, many experienced men were available for significant advisory activities in both government and industry when opportunities later expanded. The economist and the businessman came to understand and appreciate each other's contributions and points of view. Some who would have gone into academic life or stayed in federal service were given a chance to see the challenge of business, while businessmen who had thought of economists as synonymous with the worst elements of the New Deal began to see that they had some practical contribution to make. Like most developments, this change did not take place overnight. As time passed, it became clear that the prewar days would not return and that the federal-state-business relationship would become more encompassing and increasingly complex.

Many businessmen had assumed that with the end of the war and Roosevelt's death, the era of federal involvement which marked the New Deal would end. This, of course, was not to be. Not until the Eisenhower years did many people realize that the process of federal involvement was, for the moment at least, irreversible. Calvin Hoover has commented:

[8] Theodore H. White, "The Action Intellectuals," *Life*, 9 June 1967.

Many businessmen were, of course, greatly disappointed that the New Deal and Fair Deal programs were so little changed by the Eisenhower administration. Still, however much American businessmen disliked "government in business," they nevertheless felt much more relaxed and confident now that interferences with and intervention in business were in the hands of a Republican administration. Their acceptance in large part of the "New Order" as "capitalism" naturally helped to obscure recognition both in the United States and abroad of the substantial transformation of American capitalism which had in fact occurred. Communist and socialist opponents of capitalism, both in the United States and in foreign countries, of course denied that any fundamental changes had occurred. They insisted that the contemporary American economic system was undoubtedly capitalism, although a late stage characterized by monopoly instead of by competition.[9]

The value of the economist had become more obvious, and larger numbers of qualified economists were available. By 1950 men with sound professional training had spent several years rubbing elbows with their business counterparts in high-level government service. The age of the economist in business had begun.

The Economist in the Firm

If one were to ask what the major task of the industrial economist is, the answer would undoubtedly include some reference to forecasting. Of course, no one can read the future, and business economists often complain that they are not astrologers. Yet some phase of forecasting is without doubt their major activity. A firm's management is naturally interested in making some estimate of the manner in which future economic activity will influence the firm. Knowing that the gross national product is likely to increase in the coming years is of interest to an oil-producing and refining company, but it must know a great deal more. How will the increase in GNP influence the energy market, of which oil is a part? Will federal or state policy influence the output of fuels or the import of petroleum? Will imports and exports be influenced? What portion of the increasing GNP will go into purchase and operation of the motor vehicle; and of this increase, what portion can be expected to accrue to the pro-

[9] Calvin B. Hoover, *The Economy, Liberty and the State*, p. 252. © 1958 by the Twentieth Century Fund, New York.

ducer in question? In short, the company is anxious to forecast the climate or environment in which it exists.

Colin Robinson, economist for Esso Petroleum, expresses the duties of the economics division as follows:

Economics Division, then, is mainly concerned with looking at Esso's business environment and in this it is different from most other parts of the firm which are principally engaged in conducting an efficient oil business within that evironment. However, just examining the environment is in itself a useless occupation; the examination has to be translated into practical terms which the non-economist within the firm can understand. To illustrate, it is no use employing a man to make national income forecasts and then simply announcing that real GNP will rise by (say) 3 percent next year and explaining how all the expenditure components will change. Quite rightly, a firm's management wants to know what this strange fact is likely to mean in more down-to-earth terms. For example, what are the chances of balance of payments crisis? If there is such a crisis, what are the alternative ways in which this might be dealt with and which are the most likely to be applied? Is taxation on the firm's products likely to be increased? Will credit be tightened? What is the final effect on sales likely to be?[10]

The business economist is a specialist in the firm's *external relations.* More will be said about this later, but it seems quite obvious that the economist is of value chiefly to the large firm. The small firm has little use for such specialized service, although it may obtain it in "group form" from its trade association.

Economists are employed in their professional capacity by most of the leading United States firms in each field: the DuPont Company; the Chase Manhattan Bank; the Columbia Broadcasting System; Reynolds Metals Company; Goldman, Sachs & Company; Esso Standard Oil Company; Socony Mobil Oil Company; Ford Motor Company; McGraw-Hill Publishing Company; Armstrong Cork Company; SKF Industries; General Electric Company; Irving Trust Company; Union Bag, Camp Paper Company; and Bethlehem Steel Company, to name a few (for a more complete list, see Appendix B).

[10] "Economic Forecasting in the Esso Petroleum Co., Ltd.," in *The Economist in Business,* ed. by K. J. W. Alexander, A. G. Kemp, and T. M. Rybezynski (New York: Augustus M. Kelley, 1967), p. 69. See also Matthew Radom, *The Social Scientists in American Industry* (New Brunswick: Rutgers University Press, 1971).

Using more or less standard techniques, economists employed by these firms attempt to forecast the expected economic situation's influence upon the industry and upon the firm within the industry.[11]

Before examining this function in more detail, let us glance briefly at the development and nature of the economist's work in the firm. He did not come into the firm with a full-blown professional role. Some firms—notably Armstrong Cork, SKF Industries, and DuPont —were pioneers; but in most cases the economist made a gradual appearance, often "through the back door." Sales forecasting, especially for durable products and capital goods, was an obvious need. Some early forecasting work arose from the sales department's efforts to keep abreast of such matters. In other cases, capital goods outlays were the key, and the forecaster came out of and was often part of the treasurer's office. In at least one case, the economist in a large firm came from the public relations department. Having been trained in creative writing, he was put to work writing forecasts and analyses for high-level management and customer use. In earlier years few men were hired as "economists" and put into "departments of economics" per se. Titles were equally diverse. Since most were staff men, such designations as "assistant to the chairman" and "assistant to the treasurer" were often used. However, two of the pioneer companies, DuPont and Armstrong Cork, used the title "economist" or "chief economist," at least by the mid-1940s. The title, of course, reflected the status of the economist as a staff officer who was not in the line of authority. No doubt, in many cases it also reflected his often nebulous status.[12] Fortunately, most of these research positions became well entrenched, but some were ill conceived. Some executives hired economists as status symbols; others who had a legitimate need hired the wrong man, failed to give him adequate staff help, or for some reason became disenchanted with the arrangement.[13]

[11] The more widely used techniques and some major problems are discussed in William F. Butler and Robert A. Karesh, eds., *How Business Economists Forecast* (Englewood Cliffs, N.J.: Prentice-Hall, Inc., 1966).

[12] In the 1940s many business economists were "on leave" from universities, and they often remained in this status for substantial periods of time since many efforts at industrial research were short-lived. Releasing a staff assistant was much easier than abolishing a whole (though small) department.

[13] In one case called to the author's attention an economist (complete with Ph.D.) was hired in the mid-1940s by a regional restaurant chain. What the management expected is hard to imagine, but the economist soon returned to academic life. In another case, an organization asked for and got a budget item

Painful lessons were learned from this experimentation period. The firm must be large enough to use and pay an economist and his staff on a continuing basis. The management must know what to expect (no miracles), and it must outline a realistic mission. The economist must be knowledgeable about the specific industry, and he must adjust to working within the corporate framework, although he should retain a detached view and maintain his scholarly contacts.

Although his role is in flux, the business economist has more often found his niche as a forecaster or a reader of the firm's environment than as a part of the internal management team. He has made more frequent contributions in external matters than in solving managerial problems. He is more apt to concern himself with macroeconomic problems than with microeconomic problems. However, this situation is changing. Even in the past there have been notable exceptions in such areas as capital problems and the purchase of equipment. In such cases the economist has successfully lent a hand in solving internal problems. It seems more than likely that his participation in this area will increase.

MAJOR DUTIES OF THE COMPANY ECONOMIST

1. Forecasting the future environment of the firm is, as noted above, probably the major duty of the company economist. When this function has been completed, the economist is apt to step aside, leaving the decision (based in part, at least, on his forecast) to the line officers of the firm. The forecast is a useful but dangerous instrument for management to contemplate. One of the pioneer business economists notes:

The most effective use of the services of a professional economist can be made by executives who have an adequate understanding of what can be accomplished by such a person. It is also important to know what he cannot be expected to do. Because an economist can forecast sales or a change in the price of a particular material, there is no reason to promote him to the status of a wizard, swami, or crystal gazer.

Both the businessman and the economist, when engaged in making a forecast, try to understand and describe the specific results of economic and political action taken by human beings. Persons are not machines,

---

to hire an economist. However, the following year the directors reversed themselves and eliminated the funds.

and human activity in the future is not predictable in the same way that the results obtained by combining definite quantities of certain chemicals under controlled conditions are foreseeable. Anyone who makes a decision regarding what kind of a product customers will buy, how much they will purchase, how efficient competing enterprises will be in producing new products, whether inventories are high enough to justify caution in holding or increasing them, and whether or not equity prices are low relative to current earnings and prospects, is making a decision in regard to human behavior. This remains true no matter how many mathematical measurements have been used concerning the matter under consideration. Statistics dealing with economic life merely are symbols of some of the elements of a situation. The tools of the useful practicing economist are statistics of indeterminable accuracy, a knowledge of how people have acted in the past in situations which have been similar in some respects, a disciplined mind, knowledge derived as a result of critical observation, imagination, and common sense. With these instruments he endeavors to determine what people will do in the economic situations in which they will live and what the results of their activities will be.[14]

2. Reading the environment is a major task for the company economists. The firm does not exist in isolation. It is part of the national and world economies, and its actions will be influenced by changes which take place in them. The economist is by training and outlook well suited to the task of studying these factors and relating them to the firm or industry in which he is employed. Proposals regarding tariffs, fiscal and monetary policy, changes in regulatory processes, and other matters will all influence the business under consideration. The economist may pass along his judgment on these matters to his superiors in oral form, in a written report, or perhaps to the industry or public in general in an economic newsletter or bulletin. Naturally, the latter process is less satisfactory than specialized, face-to-face discussion; but for the small firm it may be all that is available.[15]

3. A third general duty is giving specific advice with regard to capital investment, marketing of a new product, defense against anti-

[14] Wilson Wright, *Forecasting for Profit* (New York: John Wiley & Sons, Inc., 1947), p. 7.
[15] Newsletters published by commercial or investment banks or firms are circulated widely, and though read by thousands of businessmen, they are of relatively little use in individual decision making. Some highly successful firms have been created since the 1930s to serve these information needs.

trust charges, and other economic problems faced by management.[16] Here the economist, working as part of the team, pools his expertise with that of lawyers, finance specialists, or others to "brainstorm" a particular problem.

It is in this function that the economist is most apt to become involved in internal managerial problems. Over a period of time he may become, in fact, part of the management team and function as a line officer.

4. The office of the economist may become the logical source of day-to-day information on sales, output, and other economic intelligence necessary to management. Staff members in the economist's office may prepare daily or weekly data sheets for the firm's management. These routine duties, supplemented by special studies, can seldom be performed by other parts of the firm because they are already burdened with their own operating duties.

5. The office of the economist should be, above all, the "think tank" or the "idea factory," a function that is admittedly somewhat in conflict with the previous one. The economist should have time to contemplate matters, read, and in general be free from administrative duties. This is, of course, only partially practicable, and it no doubt presents a constantly increasing problem to the economist who has administrative duties.[17]

Clearly, many of the economist's duties might be equally well carried on by others, and indeed, they often have been. Yet, in a sense, the economist in the firm is unique. He is trained to think in aggregate terms, and if he is properly placed within the firm, his responsibility transcends individual departments or operations. The economist must have breadth of view and should be able to visualize the problems of the firm against the problems of the economy as a whole.[18]

The expanding firm of the late nineteenth century was able to concentrate on its internal affairs with little reference to external

[16] See Peter Max, "Economics in the Courtroom," *Antitrust Law and Economics Review,* Vol. I, No. 4 (Summer, 1968), pp. 45ff.

[17] The government or academic economist may also become more administrator than economist and as a result may find himself dealing with personnel matters and travel vouchers, to the detriment of his professional work.

[18] For some interesting observations, see Robert L. Heilbroner, *The Making of Economic Society* (Englewood Cliffs, N.J.: Prentice-Hall, Inc., 1962), especially Chapt. 7.

forces. Nor surprisingly, the producer, the engineer and the technician were the key men in industrial advance. Since 1930 new forces
have come into existence, and new talents have been required for
success in the industrial system. As Daniel Fusfield notes:

> The growth of large public and private organization in the economy
> has made it clear that the impersonal operation of market forces is now
> supplemented by the ability of important groups in labor, management,
> and government to influence significantly the way the economy functions.
> Political and economic power, its organization and its locus, influence
> economic decisions as never before. Yet the new order has not developed
> an explanation of how it operates, although a suggestion was given by
> John Kenneth Galbraith in his book *American Capitalism* (1952). Gal-
> braith argued that the economic system of large organizations works ef-
> fectively only because of the existence of "countervailing power"—that
> is, one center of economic power is unable to exploit the rest of the econ-
> omy because other centers of power arise to limit its influence. Big busi-
> ness begets big labor, and large manufacturers beget large retailers and
> large suppliers of raw materials, according to Galbraith. Government
> stands as a balance wheel, ready to step in if any one economic power
> center becomes too important. In this way an orderly pattern of decision-
> making emerges out of potential chaos and conflict. Bargaining between
> small numbers of equally powerful organizations replaces the system of
> self-adjusting markets as the essential element in the economic system.
> Is this capitalism? Well, perhaps. But it is at best a greatly modified
> capitalism, quite different from the capitalism of the nineteenth century
> and earlier, and one that is continuing to change in the direction of
> larger economic units.[19]

The economist is the person in the firm most likely to deal with
these problems and to translate their meaning for others who will
have to deal with them. This is not to say that technological problems
have ceased to exist or that the engineer no longer has a role to play:
quite the contrary. Increasing technological advance is a key to
abundance, but only one key.

For more than half a century most businessmen were inclined to
ignore the force of the environment and pretended that the firm
existed in isolation. This pretense, as we have seen, ceased to be

---

[19] From *The Age of the Economist* by Daniel R. Fusfeld. Copyright © 1966
by Scott, Foresman and Company. (pp. 131–32)

viable in 1930, although most elements of business were reluctant to admit the fact. By 1950 it had become impossible to ignore the fact, and the ultimate contribution of the economist in business has been to render aid in solving the problems of the firm in this context.

Although the economist was originally a staff man and essentially a technician, he has increasingly moved into executive positions and has assumed line duties. One finds a

significant number of business economists moving into titles that include positions in planning, finance, investment, marketing, etc. It is this integration of objectives that distinguishes the successful practicing business economist from the economist who is destined to remain a specialist. Once the business economist has entered the line responsibility, there is a natural progression toward the top of the firm. An increasing number of business economists have been named senior executive officers of prominent companies, particularly financial institutions. Examples abound in the current membership directory of Federal Reserve and commercial bank presidents, and senior executive officers of manufacturing, distribution, and consulting firms. Thus, the economist is following in the tradition established by the engineer, lawyer, and accountant as professionals who have found their skills lead them to the top of major corporations. Undoubtedly, this movement will gather more momentum as the business economist gains experience within the corporation structure.[20]

Thus the economist becomes less of a specialist and more of a generalist. His professional training as such moves further into the background. Like the engineer in management who no longer uses his slide rule daily, the economist blends into the management team. As his horizion becomes broader, tasks such as forecasting grow less important.

The Economist and the Labor Union

The labor union was one of the earliest users of economic talent because, in a sense, the union deals in, manufactures, and processes economic data. Indeed, for some time the trade unions were so superior to the firms with which they dealt in performing basic eco-

[20] Herbert E. Johnson, "Presidential Address to the National Association of Business Economists" (Chicago, 25 September 1969).

nomic analysis that the business firms were forced to upgrade their own work in order to stay abreast of the unions at the bargaining table. Not surprisingly, union economists began to become active in the late 1930s when federal legislation and other developments made union activity realistic and worthwhile. If unions were to bargain with hope of success, they needed to have data on wage rates, costs of living, industrial outlooks, and related matters. As in the firm, these needs were enhanced by the entry of government into the labor-management relationship.

The fact that the union had to present an impressive public case no doubt resulted in a good deal of window dressing to support an already established goal. In the union, as in the firm and the trade association, economic analysis was widely used not only to reach a position but to justify a position already arrived at on other grounds. In the period following the Korean War, for example, unions were forced to satisfy various criteria of the stabilization authorities in order to obtain wage increases. As a result, elaborate and carefully illustrated analyses became necessary. A union in this situation had two basic goals. First, it had to establish that a wage increase was necessary in order to maintain parity. Second, it needed to show that the suggested increase would not force the industry into a price hike in order to pay it. This, of course, was a formidable task. The workers' wages had to be compared to those of comparable workers and to the various cost-of-living indices. The status of the industry or the firm had to be examined relative to others. Levels of profits, capital formation, rates of return, and other indicators of corporate health had to be compared. All this was done with full knowledge that the economists and lawyers employed by the industry would attempt to refute or belittle the union's findings. This was no task for amateurs. If the union had no talent of its own, it employed an outside consultant (the firm of Robert R. Nathan Associates was frequently used). In addition to gathering data for these presentations, it was of course necessary for the union to have accurate information for its private use.

This work was and is more often done on the home office level than on the local level. That is, the Washington office is the usual scene of such efforts. Here the economist is close to the source of raw material and can rub elbows with his fellow economists, appear at hearings, and otherwise practice his craft.

The Economist and the Trade Association

The trade association economist is a close relative (though usually on the other side of the ideological fence) of the union economist. Like the union economist, he came into demand as a result of increasing federal influence in business. There are about two hundred such groups in the Washington area. Many trade associations rose from the ruins of the National Recovery Act "code groups" after the act was struck down by the Supreme Court in 1935. The function of the trade association economist is much like that of the unionist: to gather and analyze data for internal use and to make the best possible public presentation of the industry viewpoint. Again, the work often involves presenting and defending a preconceived position. If the industry enjoys a subsidy, it must be minimized and justified in the public's mind. Also, the public service aspects of the industry must be stressed.

Perhaps the greatest contribution of trade association research efforts has been the collection of industry data. Economists who serve such bodies gather and make available data on income, employment, wage rates, and other aspects of the industry. These data are valuable to their professional colleagues. It is, of course, necessary to take these analyses with a grain of salt since the trade association economist is paid to put forth the industry viewpoint. An analysis of the economics of truck transportation and its responsibility for highway costs, made by the Association of American Railroads, for example, cannot be taken as the last word on the subject. Thus while the trade association economist may be a competent technician, it is extremely difficult for him to retain a detached point of view. As a consequence, few highly qualified professionals are attracted into such a field. Those who are generally are not highly regarded by their academic counterparts, although from time to time the academics may overcome their scruples (for a fee) and appear as expert witnesses or perform consulting work for the trade associations. Whatever his ability, the trade association economist suffers from the fact that he is an employed staff member of a highly partisan group. He cannot, by definition, take an independent line. He must be an advocate, and though perhaps a highly skilled one, an advocate nonetheless.

As one might expect, trade association economists have played the greatest role in the industries where federal policy has penetrated most deeply. Transportation, communications, and other regulated industries have a large stake in public policy. Economists who work in bodies representing these industries have made the greatest contribution and are the most highly qualified professionally.

We must not overlook the educational role played by the trade associations. Their lobbying activities are very educational, and economists have played an effective part in this work. Economists employed by trade associations either appear as witnesses at hearings or prepare economic briefs for those who do appear, and their role here has also been generally effective. Some published transcripts of hearings have become primary sources of data on the problems of an industry, thanks in no small part to economists.

Status and Working Conditions

The professional economist in business enjoys a relatively good salary and satisfactory working conditions. The rising demand for and slow increase in the number of qualified professionals in recent decades has put him in a good bargaining position.[21] Salaries generally range from $18,000 to $20,000 and upward to $30,000 for chief economists, heads of departments, and senior staff members. Status in the firm, though tenuous in the past, has been made more secure in recent years.

More young economists are being attracted into business, and formal education is becoming increasingly necessary. Informal estimates by the National Association of Business Economists indicate that about one-third of its members have the Ph.D. in economics (and this number is growing rapidly).[22] Although data are scarce, salaries seem to be somewhat higher in industrial firms than in unions and trade associations.

The separate economics department is becoming somewhat more popular, but there is still a tendency to place the economist in the

[21] See Committee on the National Science Foundation, "Structure of Economists' Employment and Salaries, 1964"; and Federal Reserve Bank of Boston, "The 7-Year Lag: The Market for Economists," *New England Business Review* (December, 1964), p. 12.

[22] The author has had helpful discussions with the executive secretary-treasurer of the NABE, Ralph E. Burgess. See Elmer G. Bratt and Milton G. Grannatt, Jr., "Survey of Business Economists," *Business Economics* (September, 1970), pp. 7ff.

office of the treasurer or some other traditional part of the firm. The department typically consists of a manager or chief economist, several subordinates, and appropriate nonprofessional staff. In large departments work is organized by function, but more often the staff works on an informal basis with all parties lending a hand where necessary.

Over the years the economist has essentially made a job for himself by demonstrating his expertise. In one case familiar to the author, for example, the economist originally hired was a young man with modest professional training. He was viewed by the top management as a data gatherer and an adjunct to the general office staff. Neither party was pleased, and after some time the economist resigned. The job remained unfilled for a time and was then taken by an experienced man who quickly built the position into one of stature in the organization, performing a useful and highly professional function. Most business economists now alive have seen their present jobs created in this manner, either by themselves or their immediate predecessors.[23]

Professional Training and Outlook

Data are also scarce in this area, but two facts seem to stand out: (1) many, if not most, of the senior economists have not had systematic professional training leading to the terminal degree, and (2) the younger economists now moving into business more often have had such training.

This situation, of course, reflects the growing professionalism and specialization of economic training. Whereas the classical academic economist attempted to answer broad questions by constructing comprehensive theories, the modern economist concentrates on more specialized and operationally feasible problems. The implications of this change have been well put by E. Ray Canterbery:

The study of economics is today at another turning point. In the past twenty years economists have become increasingly more professional as economics has become more systematized. Financial and economic data necessary for expanded economic knowledge are being provided by many

[23] Many of the pioneers are still on the job, but the second generation is rising rapidly. Few business economists were in office before 1940, although a dozen or so have been identified.

governmental agencies, private research foundations, and economics, departments of colleges and universities. Economic indices, such as steel ingot output, carloadings, retail sales, business failures, industrial materials prices, personal income, etc., are reported weekly. Developments in economic analysis, national income accounting, and data processing now contribute to a better understanding and prediction of the impact of various business and financial transactions upon specific industries. . . .

The individual economist cannot be master of all branches of this expanded knowledge. The modern economist is a specialist, concentrating on one segment of an economy. . . . Consequently, he is today more useful to business. . . .

The modern economist is more skilled analyzing commodities markets than the behavior of men. Economists are employed even by advertising, the industry that allegedly manipulates human desires. Those with such skills in advertising agencies are usually market researchers on industrial or agricultural accounts. Because the economist is most at home studying national economic trends, he is useful in predicting market trends for the products of industries which largely determine or are determined by the course of the total economy, such as automobiles and steel.[24]

In addition, the modern economist interested in business is more in tune with accountants, management specialists, computer programmers, and others on the management team. The traditional split between economists in academic life and business administration types is less noticeable than it was two decades ago. As growing numbers of professionals enter the business world, this trend toward a community of interest can be expected to continue.

Professional Problems of the Business Economist

During the many years in which economists were concerned almost entirely with academic affairs, ethical problems were those of the scholar. In summing up this situation, George Terbrough notes:

Historically, the economics profession developed in the cloister. Until the last generation the overwhelming majority of its practitioners were academicians. Its professional ethics, in consequence, have been the ethics of the scholar and the scientist, demanding complete honesty and integrity at all times.

As the profession has emerged from the cloister into government and

[24] "The Diminishing Uselessness of Economists in Business," *Mississippi Valley Journal of Business and Economics,* Vol. I, No. 1 (Fall, 1965), p. 6.

business, it has found itself pressed increasingly into the role of mouth-piece for nonacademic employers—in short, into a role of advocacy. In-creasingly, its members appear in a representative capacity, as economic brief writers, organization spokesmen, expert witnesses. Yet the profes-sion has not evolved a code of ethics appropriate to these new respon-sibilities. Officially, it still retains the obligation of the scholar for com-plete honesty and objectivity. The result is a compromising and ambigu-ous situation, embarrassing to the economist and sometimes even to his client.[25]

M. J. Rossant is critical of economists in this regard, for in his view, they expect to be free of criticism when they engage in ad-vocacy.

It is possible, of course, to achieve peace of mind, to convince oneself that the kind of job that is being done serves both the truth and the employer. But as a journalist, cynical by nature and by craft, I question it. And my questioning leads me to believe that economists must be aware that they cannot enter the kitchen, as President Truman so pun-gently put it, unless they are prepared to stand the heat.

In my view, economists have not yet recognized this elemental fact of life. They seem to believe that they can flaunt that basic law that holds you cannot have your cake and eat it too. But once an economist speaks on behalf of a political party or a business firm, it seems to me that he no longer can be considered the purveyor of an independent viewpoint. I may be harsh in this judgment but it is no harder to treat economists in such fashion than it is to treat lawyers, accountants, historians or nuclear physicists who for prestige or profit agree to represent a par-ticular view.

Yet my real concern about ethics goes much deeper. Simply because economists have come of age and are reaping the honors and prizes and the emoluments of public respect and approval, economists are under a growing obligation to do honest and painstaking work. But is this really the case? I am forced to doubt it. I find, for example, that much of the work done by economists is shoddy and pedestrian, often begged, bor-rowed or stolen, rather than clean and original.[26]

[25] "Ethics of Advocacy," *Business Economics*, Vol. II, No. 1 (Fall, 1956), p. 18. See also Walter E. Hoadley, "Ethical Problems of the Economist in His Firm," *Business Economics*, Vol. II, No. 1 (Fall, 1956); and M. J. Rossant, "Ethics in the Age of the Economist," *Business Economics*, Vol. II, No. 1 (Fall, 1956).
[26] Rossant, "Ethics in the Age of the Economist," pp. 20–21.

Although he is critical, Rossant sees no gain and perhaps loss from the adoption of an ethical code similar to those of other professions.

While I am concerned about these problems I do not think that they can be solved by an explicit code of conduct. To be sure, a code may confer a certain amount of professional status but it does not seem to me that economists are suffering from a low level of recognition or respect. Indeed, they might invite suspicions and provoke hostility by establishing rigid rules of conduct that would inevitably make the profession appear to outsiders as being much more exclusive and protective than it is now. While other learned professions may require adherence to formal codes I am not altogether sure that the public benefits; too often, they are used to serve the special interests of professionals.[27]

These problems, like those of the government economist, are far from solved. Yet the fact that business economists are considering them and are aware of their implications is a great step in the right direction.

The Consultants

Private consultants are of many types and varieties and have widely diverse backgrounds. Because no procedure for licensing is required, anyone who wishes to may "hang out his shingle" as a consulting economist.[28] Consulting "firms" range from the one-man enterprise operating from a Washington apartment or from shared desk space in a low-rent building to the large, well-financed firm engaged in worldwide operations.

Some general classification of these firms will illustrate the usual modes of organization and operation.

TYPES OF FIRMS

Perhaps the best known are the large, well-established firms which are generally based in New York or Washington, D.C. Such firms are soundly financed and engage in work of many types.[29] These

---

[27] *Ibid.*, p. 21.

[28] In most states engineers, investment counselors, and most other types of consultants must be licensed, although training requirements are very lax.

[29] The firms discussed here are those devoted to consulting in economics. However, economists also play a large role in firms devoted to engineering (generally management) and other types of business consulting services. See

firms have numerous contracts in force with both government and private corporations.[30] Their work covers many areas, and they produce both specialized and general studies. Other firms are similar in character but restrict their efforts to studies in transportation, public finance, or some other specific field. Both types of firms share common characteristics and differ only in the kind of work in which they engage.

The organization generally consists of a principal who lends his name to the group and a number of partners or associates who have a financial interest in the firm, participate in its management, and share its profits or losses. These firms may have anywhere from a handful to several hundred professional staff members and an appropriate number of supporting personnel. Since such a firm requires considerable office space (impressive enough to attract favor from clients), and travel funds, overhead expenses are substantial. Revenue comes only from research projects; thus a constant stream of proposals must be forthcoming, and the firm must have sufficient resources to weather slack periods. A given project may last for many months, but it is common for periodic payments to be made upon proof of progress. Thus the firm need not wait for payment until the whole job is done.

The consulting business has been a growth industry since the Second World War, and competition continues to increase rapidly. Consulting firms have proliferated, both through the establishment of new enterprises and through the entry of firms long established in other fields.[31] The resulting competition has led to a large number of mergers. While the well-entrenched firm often has substantial advantages, the existence of even the oldest firm is often precarious.

The consulting firm is also a highly personal organization, and the senior principal is a figure of importance. Hence, his death or retirement may force a drastic reorganization and in many cases puts the firm out of business.

W. F. Lutrell, "The Work of an Economic Consultant: The Economist in Business," in *The Economist in Business*, ed. by K. J. W. Alexander, A. G. Kelley, and T. M. Rybezynski (New York: Augustus M. Kelley, 1967), pp. 163ff.

[30] Large firms are increasingly occupied with foreign assignments, either directly or through a consortium.

[31] Public accounting and general management consultants have increasingly moved into economic consulting since 1950.

Research money is often the first to be eliminated from the budgets of both public and private institutions, and what was a lush market can dry up rapidly. Cuts in federal spending may, for example, be fatal to such firms. The mortality rate of consulting firms is extremely high for these reasons and also because they are often established with totally inadequate financial resources. However, most of the successful firms now in operation have grown from humble beginnings. Many large Washington firms now located in impressive buildings on K Street and Connecticut Avenue originated some twenty years ago in shared offices in far less impressive buildings.

In addition to the large, well-established firms, two types of small organizations exist in great numbers: one-man firms engaged in full-time consulting and one-man firms operating on a part-time basis. Again, these firms are similar. The small firm is most often specialized, and it frequently lacks the resources necessary to seek major contracts (a proposal alone may mean an outlay of many thousands of dollars). As a consequence, these firms often subcontract through larger operations.

In planning this chapter, the author had an understandable desire to indicate the number of firms engaged in consulting. The fact that this venture foundered is illustrative of the basic problem: what is an economic consulting firm? Is the one-man or part-time operation to be included? Are management consulting and engineering firms to be included since they often engage in economic studies? If one includes the established, full-time firms that specialize in economic work, have offices in commercial buildings (not in the home), and employ ten or more full-time workers, the list is probably less than two dozen. If one counts the informally established "firms" and those engaged essentially in management or engineering consulting and accounting, the list grows to several thousand.[32] The 1969 *Washington Telephone Classified Directory* lists twenty-five or thirty consulting economists. Several of these are nationally known, well-

---

[32] See Paul Wasserman and Willis P. Greer, *Consultants and Consulting Organizations* (Ithaca: Cornell University Graduate School of Business and Public Administration, 1969). This publication attempts to list all organizations and tries to segregate them according to interest. It is clear, however, that many list themselves as qualified in economics in order to cover all areas. There were 581 in all—47 in Washington and 90 in New York City.

established firms. Others are clearly one-man, residence-based operations.[33]

It would, of course, be possible to apply various criteria to determine what constitutes a bona fide firm—length of time in business, gross income from professional activities, number of contracts in force, number of full-time employees, and location of offices, for example. No such tests are applied, and being in business is largely a matter of having letterheads printed or listing oneself in the "yellow pages."

One matter deserves comment, however. The quality of a product does not always correlate with other factors. Although the one-man firm cannot engage in projects requiring a nationwide organization, it may often perform with considerable efficiency. An office with impressive furniture in a modern building does not always guarantee a sound report.

Consulting firms, like other businesses, have passed through stages of increasing scale, and the one-man operations now face more difficult competition.[34] Yet they survive; and in a sense, one-man, part-time operations are probably the most numerous.

College professors in urban areas frequently engage in part-time consulting as individuals, as members of a group, or as consultants to established firms on a per diem basis. In the Washington, D.C. area, the ranks of one-man firms also include retired federal and trade association economists who market their expertise and exploit their former contacts to supplement their retirement incomes. These persons also provide a supply of staff members for the large firms. Although age sometimes limits their "second careers," federal employees often retire at a relatively young age and thus enjoy fifteen or twenty more productive years. The disadvantage of age is often offset by "know how" and contacts in the proper places.

For tax purposes and other reasons, consulting activity is most

[33] One "firm," for example, has an address which might be either commercial or residential. The quarters are, in fact, both. The principal and sole member of the firm (a retired federal employee) conducts business without the aid of a secretary. All correspondence is hand written. It is hard to guess what the firm's income is, but it is clearly modest.

[34] Naturally, the client wants some indication of how his job will be done, and the best gauge is the quality and experience of the staff. Thus the well-established firm will be more apt to get contracts since they have more experience; and the more contracts they get, the more experience they build up.

often formally organized into a "firm," the partnership being a common form. Earnings vary widely. One-man firms may earn anywhere from nothing to several thousand dollars yearly. For reasons which are not clear, the quality of work often seems to bear little relationship to the financial success of the firm, at least in the short run. Perhaps the amount of research work being done is so great that any established firm can obtain contracts. Or perhaps a more likely reason is that many problems are so poorly defined that any answer is a good answer. One factor is clear: the number of "economists" engaged in research, either on their own or as employees of consulting firms, far exceeds the number who can be considered professionally qualified by any acceptable standard. One cannot escape the fact that many consulting firms deal in a superficial product and that a major "housecleaning" would probably be beneficial. It would also be very helpful if qualifications for practice were established. Though such standards seem to be very far in the future, no doubt they will be established. Consulting economists, like lawyers, accountants, and engineers, will then be required to pass suitable examinations and meet prescribed educational standards.

CLIENTS AND TYPE OF WORK

Clients of economic consultants are, like the firms themselves, diverse. Federal, state, and local governments require a wide variety of economic studies and provide a major portion of the market for consultants' services. As we have seen, even when business firms, trade associations, and labor unions employ economists of their own, they often require outside aid or wish to obtain a fresh viewpoint and thus have recourse to private consultants.

For most economic consultants the number and type of clients is limited by the type of work performed. Broad guage projects such as economic base studies are desired not so much by the individual firm as by governmental units and such organizations as trade associations and chambers of commerce. Retail firms desiring market research studies, for example, would be likely to seek out specialists in the area and would seldom employ consulting economists.

The great increase in governmental problems coupled with growing federal and state responsibility in such complex areas as defense, economic development, and poverty has vastly increased the demand for these studies. Programs for economic development in Appalachia and the Coastal Plains and the many projects involving foreign aid, for example, require serious study before intelligent solutions can be formulated.

QUALITIES OF THE CONSULTANT

The organization employing a consulting firm does so for obvious reasons. It needs the firm's expert knowledge and experience, which it lacks either entirely or in part.

The consulting firm has a thin layer of top talent. It is a highly personal business. The principal is a man of reputation, and the client feels slighted unless the principal makes at least a pretense of supervising his particular project. Clearly, this is impossible in a large firm. The organization of work becomes very difficult, and deadlines are constantly pressing. Consequently, the success of the firm often carries its own seeds of destruction. The principal spends his time in hotels or on airplanes, and if talent is not available at the lower levels, the work suffers.

One of the major advantages of the consulting firm is that it is often able to approach the problem with a fresh viewpoint. Thus it may see points which the client has overlooked. The consultant can avoid his client's professional myopia. Another advantage which the consultant brings to bear upon the problem is his breadth of experience. Most problems are related; and the economist, like the lawyer or engineer, can employ his experience in cases A and B to throw light on cases C, D, and N.

THE ECONOMICS OF THE CONSULTING ECONOMIST

Unlike the business economist who is employed by the firm, the consultant works on a fee basis, either by the job or per diem (generally the former if he is a member of a firm and the latter if he works alone). Professional and nonprofessional effort is the major element of cost. Compared to other businesses, the consulting firm has modest capital investments (office space is rented and furniture and office equipment can be leased), very modest costs for materials (paper, printing, etc.), and of course, no inventory.[35] Fees for a major project may amount to several hundred thousand dollars or more. Per diem fees are variable and range from one hundred to more than five hundred dollars per day depending upon the location, the necessity for court appearances, and such factors

[35] This does not include files of past cases—a very valuable item in the consultant's trade but of little value in the usual sense.

as the name and reputation of the consultant. An established scholar of high repute in the field can be more valuable and can charge more than an equally capable man who is not widely known.

The initial investment is modest, though more than is often thought, and a successful firm becomes a profitable, though uncertain, enterprise. It is difficult to set specific figures, but a year's lease on an office and equipment and enough money to pay salaries, telephone bills, and travel expenses would be required. Perhaps seventy-five to one hundred thousand dollars, depending upon the situation, would be needed as initial capital. Though no data are available, more firms probably have failed than have succeeded.

The greatest element of risk probably lies in the fact that available work is apt to fluctuate greatly, giving the business a "feast or famine" quality. This is a particular problem if the firm must secure outside personnel, which is often the case. Academic people, for example, must be given assurance of employment if they are to take leave from their teaching posts. If, for instance, a proposal is made in July and the firm arranges for an academic person to take leave from September through January to serve on the project, he will have to be compensated even if the proposal is not accepted since he has cut himself off from his regular source of income. There are also apt to be long "dry spells" when, despite a lack of income, the organization must be kept together, rent must be paid, and other expenses must be met.

These factors make consulting a precarious business. They also tend to expand the firm's scale and diversify its range of operations. An effort is made to keep a steady flow of projects. This of course means more bids and proposals and necessitates a greater range of capabilities. A fair amount of wasted effort is generated since the firm must keep its name in the field and therefore often bids on projects with little hope of actually landing the job. However, the critical issue is usually personnel. Since the firm is selling a service, it must stud the proposal with impressive names; and because these people are in short supply, the effort to spread them as thin as possible is continual and often fatal.[36]

[36] There is a great deal of interfirm exchange of information, and most firms know who is bidding on what projects at any given time. Highly specialized projects are often conceded as unsuitable to all but one or two firms, or perhaps a joint effort is necessary.

The National Association of Business Economists

As the number of economists engaged in business increased, those who were concerned entirely or chiefly with such activities found the American Economic Association an inadequate forum for their needs. The AEA had always been largely academic in tone, which is understandable since most of its membership was academic. As a result, the National Association of Business Economists was founded in 1959 to meet the:

professional needs of the rapidly growing number of business economists. The Association meets annually in September and also sponsors several seminars each year on special topics of interest to the membership.

The official journal of the National Association of Business Economists is *Business Economics* which is published four times a year and which contains papers delivered at the annual meetings and seminars as well as other articles of interest to business economists.[37]

By 1970 the NABE had some 1,500 members and had become a growing influence. A major feature of the annual meeting is the *NABE Survey*, a forecast of economic events. The survey itself, in which some two hundred NABE members participate, draws considerable national attention. Most NABE members are also members of the AEA, and of course, a number of economists who are essentially academic but also engage in consulting are NABE members.

As economists have moved into business, a winnowing process has taken place. The more pragmatic types have selected careers in business, and the academicians have remained on the campus. Fortunately for the whole profession, a fair number have been interested and capable in both worlds.

In a stimulating paper recently delivered to the Southern Economic Association, Leonard S. Silk of the Brookings Institution raised interesting questions about the relationship between the business economist and his more cloistered brethren. He speculates that in general the academic economist is apt to be more competent than his counterpart in business:

I hesitate to offer a personal judgment rather than data to establish the relative competence of academic versus business economists. But

---

[37] National Association of Business Economists, *Business Economics Careers* (Washington, D.C.: National Association of Business Economists, 1968), p. 16.

since I have no data, based either on tests of economic understanding, such as we give to high school and college students and teachers *en masse*, or on a detailed evaluation of the performance of economists as analysts, forecasters, and policy advisors. I can offer only a personal guess. Let me formulate my guess as follows: Suppose that I were staffing *any* economic project, within business, government, or an academic institution and could have my choice among the top 100 academic economists and among the top 100 business economists, how would I rate candidates in terms of their capabilities, if I wanted a choice list of no more than 20 names? My guess is that I would come out with at least 15 academicians and no better than 5 business economists. You might try that test for yourself. Professional decorum prevents me from naming names, but, before I am accused of arrant bias in favor of the academics (or excessive generosity toward the business economists), I suggest that you try to draw up your own list. And when that first list is done, ask yourself how you would choose if you had to assemble another 20-man list from a second batch—the 100 *next* best academicians and the 100 *next* best business economists. My personal experiences in the realms of academia and business would lead me to say that the second batch would show even more clearly the better training, sharper mathematical and statistical tool-using ability, superior ability to organize complex research, and wider ranging imaginativeness of the academic contingent.[38]

Silk notes, however, that the balance is shifting and that the business contingent is growing in overall competence.

In contrast with his leisurely move from the classroom into government, the economist's rise in the firm has been rapid. The full implications are yet to be seen. Lawyers, accountants, and engineers can be used in large numbers, but economists (especially those at high levels) are likely to remain limited in number.

The increasing use of the professional economist in business is especially interesting since it was the most difficult area for him to enter. Long after the economist had made a place in public service, the businessman remained unconvinced that he had any real contribution to make. It was not until the Second World War that the economist began to breach this wall, but by 1970 business employment had begun to overtake government as a market for the economist's services.

[38] Leonard S. Silk, "The Business Economist and the Academic Economist," paper delivered 13 November 1969 to the Thirty-ninth Annual Conference of the Southern Economic Association, St. Louis. Mimeographed.

6
By Way of Summary

OUR task in this book has been to examine and evaluate the expanding role of the professional economist. Economics as a science is roughly two centuries old. Adam Smith published *An Inquiry into the Nature and Causes of the Wealth of Nations* in 1776. Like most economists of the future, Smith was an academician and never held public office; yet his work had enormous impact. For many years thereafter academic economists were reluctant to leave the campus, and the gulf between academicians and men of affairs became increasingly broad. Now, almost two hundred years later, economists throughout the world have emerged from academia into the world of government and business.

In terms of the sweep of history, this change has taken but a moment. Yet it has not been accomplished with ease. The rise of the economist and his increasing recognition by society has resulted from significant changes within and outside the profession. Before we examine the implications of the economist's new status, let us review briefly the factors underlying his increasing acceptance.

The New Economics and the New Economists

Since 1920 major changes have taken place within the profession. The foundations of the present-day system of economic analysis and advice were laid in private research organizations and governmental agencies between 1930 and 1945. The National Bureau of Economic Research, the Bureau of the Budget, the Department of Commerce, the Office of Price Administration, and the Defense Department were coequal with the universities as training schools for the "new economics." This change has been slow, and probably few other than the professional economists appreciate its magnitude. National income analysis, input-output analysis, and other tools of modern economics useful in government and business were, to all intents, nonexistent before the Second World War. The critical need for rational wartime planning intensified their development. The economist's contribution during the stressful war years assured his participation in the postwar era in both government and industry.[1] The government's involvement in business since 1945 has made much the same type of economic analysis mandatory from the standpoint of the government and those subject to governmental policy.

In contrast with their somewhat pedestrian performance in the field during the depression years, economists have generally been able to respond to these needs. When one considers that the professional economist had been in existence in some form for almost half a century by 1935, it would appear that the profession was woefully short on practical solutions to actual problems. Yet in a span of a few years, economists apparently were able to make a satisfactory contribution. What was the cause of this change? Was the "Keynesian Revolution" such a mighty force that it changed the outlook and ability of an entire profession?[2] Or were the problems of wartime economics, although tremendous in scope, more easily approached than those of the depression? It cannot be denied that the wartime problems fell more within the competence of micro-oriented economists than did those of the depression.

---

[1] Former Secretary of State Dean Acheson has noted the contribution of wartime economists associated with the Board of Economic Warfare in the confusing period just before and after the U.S. entry into World War II. See Dean G. Acheson, *Present at the Creation* (New York: W. W. Norton & Co., 1969), pp. 43ff.

[2] The overthrow of Say's Law by the wide acceptance of Keynes's General Theory was to be a powerful factor in the state's increased responsibility for assuring full employment. This was one factor leading to the need for planning, which in turn led to a need for economic analysis; but it would be difficult to assign great weight to this factor. See Paul Baran, "National Economic Planning," in *A Survey of Contemporary Economics*, ed. by Bernard F. Haley, Vol. 2, American Economic Association (Homewood, Ill.: Richard D. Irwin, 1952), pp. 355–403. For a fine analysis and appraisal of Keynesian economics and its influence on policy after thirty years see Alvin Hansen, "Keynes After Thirty Years (With Reference to the United States)," *Weltwirtshaftlicher Archives*, Band 97, Heftz, 1966, pp. 15–27.

Keynesian economics was taking hold in leading American universities by the late 1930s, but one can assume that most of the mature economists who were active during World War II had been trained in earlier years. The present (1970s) leaders of the profession were just emerging from graduate school in 1940. Most price control, allocation, and other economic problems incident to war were probably handled at the policy level by older economists whose training had been pre-Keynesian. To the extent that this was true, microeconomic thinking was probably dominant. Since 1940 the body of economic doctrine has become more cohesive, more standardized, and more systematized. In short, economics, at least in its academic branches, has become more of a science.

We take it for granted that economics has made progress toward the goal of status as a systematic science since 1920 or even 1940, that the increasing sophistication of mathematics has to a degree made it more exact and increased the usefulness of the tool kit, and that the economists who perform with success in the firm or the government are often among the most able in the profession.[3] Do these factors explain the increasing success and prestige of the economist outside academic life; and more precisely, do they explain the change which seemingly took place in the short period between 1935 and 1945? Apparently they do when one recalls that these factors were acting in concert.

This new status was most visible in the realm of public policy. Nonetheless, in his presidential address to the American Economic Association in 1964 (at the height of the discussion about the "new economics"), George Stigler commented on the pitfalls of policy making:

On what basis have economists felt themselves equipped to give useful advice on the proper functions of the state? By what methods did Smith and his disciples show the incapacity of the state in economic affairs? By what methods did later economists who favored state control of railroads, stock exchanges, wage rates and prices, farm output, and a thousand other things, prove that these were better directed or operated by the state? How does an economist acquire as much confidence in the

[3] That is, these economists are able in the "can do" sense and not necessarily as scholars or theoreticians. Many of the great academic thinkers would fail to survive in government or business since they lack the personal qualities necessary to succeed in such a situation.

wisdom of a policy of free trade or fiscal stabilization as he has in the law of diminishing returns of the profit-maximizing propensities of entre-preneurs?

The thought behind these questions is simple. Economists generally share the ruling values of their societies, but their professional compe-tence does not consist in translating popular wishes into an awe-inspiring professional language. Their competence consists in understanding how an economic system works under alternative institutional frameworks. If they have anything of their own to contribute to the popular discussion of economic policy, it is some special understanding of the relationship between policies and results of policies.

The basic role of the scientist in public policy, therefore, is that of establishing the costs and benefits of alternative institutional arrange-ments. Smith had no professional right to advise England on the Naviga-tions Acts unless he had evidence of their effects and the probable effects of their repeal. A modern economist has no professional right to advise the federal government to regulate or deregulate the railroads unless he has evidence of the effects of these policies. . . .

The essential ambiguity of general theoretical systems with respect to public policy, however, has been the real basis of our troubles. So long as a competent economist can bend the existing theory to either side of most viable controversies without violating the rules of profes-sional work, the voice of the economist must be a whisper in the legisla-tive halls.[4]

Many of these problems remain to be solved, for as yet the econo-mist has merely put a foot into the door of public policy and has mastered only the simplest of tools of analysis. Nonetheless, his status in the world of affairs is much different than it was half a century ago.

The new economist has enjoyed the recognition of his peers and has basked in the glow of success on the national scene.[5] The success-

---

[4] "The Economist and the State," *American Economic Review*, Vol. LV, No. 1 (March, 1965), p. 13.

[5] An interesting though informal index of influence is the appearance of economists in the mass media. *Time*, for example, has featured economists in its lead story. The December 19, 1969 issue, for instance, dealt with Milton Friedman, a University of Chicago professor who holds no public office but is of national influence. Heller, Keynes (in 1965, nineteen years after his death), and others have appeared on *Time*'s cover. Friedman and Paul Samuelson write regular columns for *Newsweek*, and *Time* has a regular panel of econo-mists. Heller, of course, was a public official, but the others have been private citizens.

ful "economic engineering" underlying the tax cut in 1964 made him a political hero, and he was widely applauded by the businessmen who long looked with suspicion on all his works.

Equally important, the economist has shed his traditional reluctance to make his voice heard in the goal-setting process. Viewing himself as an academic scientist, the economist was reluctant to become involved in the process of selecting ends and attempted to confine himself to means. He is increasingly less willing to say, "Show me what ends are to be achieved, and I will use my expertise to achieve them." He now more often says, "I want a voice in the choice of goals as well as a role in the technical process of achieving them." He must play the roles of citizen and economist. To some extent he must merge these roles and to a degree, keep them separate.

In his role as educator, the economist may point out the alternatives of various policy actions; but as a participant in policy making —as government official, businessman, citizen, or adviser—he must act on these matters in concert with his fellow citizens. He has duties both as an informed professional and as a participating citizen with gains and losses to calculate on a personal basis. As a professional he has more expertise than his fellow citizens. Therefore, he has a greater responsibility to use his talents, though as a citizen he has no more authority than others. His knowledge can never be perfect, and he may make errors.

Nevertheless, the social scientist can make important contributions to the discussion of objectives. He can point out, for instance, that many things that people think are ends are in fact means to some further end, and that a discussion that seems to be about ends may be more easily resolved if it can be stated in terms of a choice of means to some further end. He may also usefully point out that human activity seldom has but one objective, and that there are many ends, some of which may not be compatible. We want peace, but we do not want the things that make for peace; we want health, but we do not want the things that make for health; we want riches, but we also want things that make for poverty.[6]

Perhaps in the past the economist has tried too hard to be "scientific" and "detached," an observer but not a participant. His in-

---

[6] Kenneth Boulding, *Principles of Economic Policy* (Englewood Cliffs, N.J.: Prentice-Hall, Inc., 1958), p. 2. © 1958, Prentice-Hall, Inc.

creasing visibility has made this impossible. The economist cannot have it both ways. If he wants to stay in the ivory tower, good enough; but if he wants to continue his move into the outside world, he must be prepared to take stands on issues of the day and to defend them professionally.

Lionel Robbins, a professor at the London School of Economics, notes that the age of involvement has arrived:

I say nothing against the attitude of specialization and detachment; it is one of the glories of a free society that it allows such things to be. It is one of its advantages too; in the end the advancement of practical knowledge owes much to the remote and to the eccentric. Nevertheless, in my opinion, it would be a great pity if economists in the present age were to depart from the habits of their predecessors and to refrain from participation in the discussion of what, to use the old term, may conveniently be described as questions of political economy. I think it would be regrettable if they refrained from discussions of the ultimate ends of society.[7]

Ragnar Frisch (a first-rate theoretician and Nobel Prize winner) has made much the same point. The overly cautious attitude of the economist has brought him needless difficulties. Others have not hesitated to enter where he has been so reluctant to tread. Engineers, journalists, businessmen, and those with slender economic credentials have shown little hesitation about making definitive economic statements. One can hope, and with some reason, that the increasingly professional and homogeneous training which younger economists now receive will be a major factor in the field's future professionalism.[8]

The Moral Commitment

Increasing involvement brings rewards but also a wide range of practical and philosophical problems. Kenneth Boulding, in his 1969 presidential address before the American Economic Association,

[7] Lionel Robbins, *The Economist in the Twentieth Century* (London: Macmillan Co., Ltd., 1954), pp. 15–16. © 1954 Macmillan Co. and St. Martins Press. See also Lionel Robbins, *Autobiography of an Economist* (London: Macmillan Co., Ltd., 1971).

[8] Ragnar Frisch, *Theory of Production* (Dordrech-Holland: D. Reidel Publishing Co., and Chicago: Rand McNally & Co., 1965), pp. 7–8.

suggested a return to the "moral science" approach which originally characterized the field.

Boulding devotes much attention to the scientific apparatus of economics and the construction of value systems which, though accepted by most economists, in his view rest on "an extremely shaky foundation of ethical propositions."

No one in his senses would want his daughter to marry an economic man, one who counted every cost and asked for every reward, was never afflicted with mad generosity or uncalculating love, and who never acted out of a sense of inner identity and indeed had no inner identity even if he was occasionally affected by carefully calculated considerations of benevolence or malevolence. The attack on economics is an attack on calculatedness and the very fact that we think of the calculating as cold suggests how exposed economists are to romantic and heroic criticism.[9]

Would one indeed want his daughter to marry the classic "economic man"? Of course, one would be repelled by such a suggestion. Economics must be more than costs and benefits measured in dollar terms, even though it must concern itself with such matters. Its primary concern must be the welfare of society.

Thus the very progress of the economist in making his field more precise and more scientific has, in one sense, come to little. His ability to participate in the real world of government and industry has largely been realized, but he must now set newer and broader goals. Much of his present status in both business and government has been based on narrow technical expertise. Many of the broad, humanistic issues have been put aside as being outside the economist's area of concern or as too troublesome. This practice must cease if he wishes to make a continuing contribution.

Economists, though they represent one of the smallest professions, have influence in society far beyond their numbers. As teachers and advisers to policy makers, their influence is unique. Influence implies responsibility not only for technical expertise but to use one's influence in a constructive fashion for human welfare. May the economist, as he looks back upon his accomplishments, look forward to his opportunities to serve mankind.

[9] "Presidential Address, American Economic Association, 1969," *American Economic Review*, Vol. LIX, No. 1 (March, 1969), pp. 1–12.

Appendixes

APPENDIX A
Some Outstanding Economists

Academicians of Distinction

The following economists are distinguished among their peers, but there are many others who might be listed. For obvious reasons, the author has made no attempt to survey the profession on a systematic basis. Those listed were living in 1970.

Moses Abromovitz	Stanford
Kenneth Arrow[a]	Stanford
Joe S. Bain	California (Berkeley)
William J. Baumol	Princeton
Gary Becker[a]	Columbia
Kenneth Boulding[a]	Colorado
Arthur F. Burns	Columbia, federal service, CEA
Evsey Domar	MIT
James Duesenberry	Harvard
William J. Fellner[a]	Yale
Milton Friedman[a]	Chicago
John Kenneth Galbraith	Harvard
Alexander Gerschenkron[b]	Harvard
Zvi Griliches[a]	Chicago
Gottfried Haberler	Harvard
Walter W. Heller	Minnesota, CEA
Harold Hoteling[b]	North Carolina
Hendrick Houthakker	Harvard
Harry G. Johnson	Chicago, London
Dale Jorgenson[a]	Harvard
Lawrence Klein[a]	Pennsylvania
Frank H. Knight[c]	Chicago
Simon Kuznets	Harvard

141

Wassily Leontief	MIT
Abba P. Lerner[b]	California (Berkeley)
Fritz Machlup	Princeton
Jacob Marschak[b]	California (Los Angeles)
Edward S. Mason	Harvard
Lloyd A. Metzler	Chicago
Franco Modigliani	MIT
Richard Nelson	Yale
Marc Nerlove[a]	Chicago
Paul Samuelson[a]	MIT (Nobel Prize, 1970)
Theodore Schultz	Chicago
Arthur Smithies	Harvard
Robert M. Solow[a]	MIT
Joseph Spengler	Duke
George Stigler	Chicago
James Tobin[a]	Yale
Robert Triffin	Yale
Jacob Viner[c]	Princeton
Ludwig Von Mises[b]	Institute for Advanced Study

[a] John Bates Clark Medal winner.
[b] AEA, Distinguished Fellow.
[c] Francis A. Walker Medal winner.

LIVING PAST PRESIDENTS OF THE AMERICAN ECONOMIC ASSOCIATION

Walter F. Willcox	Cornell	**1915**
John M. Clark	Columbia	**1935**
Alvin S. Johnson	New School	**1936**
Alvin H. Hansen	Harvard	**1938**
Jacob Viner	Chicago	**1939**
Frederick C. Mills	Columbia	**1940**
Edwin G. Nourse	Brookings	**1942**
Albert B. Wolfe	Ohio State	**1943**
Joseph S. Davis	Stanford	**1944**
I. L. Sharfman	Michigan	**1945**
Paul H. Douglas	Chicago	**1947**
Howard S. Ellis	California	**1949**
Frank H. Knight	Chicago	**1950**
John H. Williams	Harvard	**1951**
Calvin B. Hoover	Duke	**1953**
Simon Kuznets	Pennsylvania	**1954**

Morris A. Copeland	Cornell	1957
George W. Stocking	Vanderbilt	1958
Arthur F. Burns	Columbia	1959
Theodore W. Schultz	Chicago	1960
Paul A. Samuelson	MIT	1961
Edward S. Mason	Harvard	1962
Gottfried Haberler	Harvard	1963
George J. Stigler	Chicago	1964
Joseph J. Spengler	Duke	1965
Fritz Machlup	Princeton	1966
Milton Friedman	Chicago	1967
Kenneth E. Boulding	Colorado	1968
William J. Fellner	Yale	1969
Wassily Leontiff	Harvard	1970
James Tobin	Yale	1971
John Kenneth Galbraith	Harvard	1972
Kenneth Arrow	Harvard	1973

Prominent Business Economists

Any list of well-known business economists would include Wilson Wright, a pioneer business economist with Armstrong Cork Co. (now retired); the late Adolph Abramson of SKF Industries; Herbert E. Johnson of Continental Illinois Bank and Trust Co.; Allan Greenspan of Townsend, Greenspan & Company; Charles B. Reeder of E. I. DuPont de Nemours & Company; and Ralph E. Burgess of the National Association of Securities Dealers, Inc. The following men have been honored by the NABE and were living in 1970.

NATIONAL ASSOCIATION OF BUSINESS ECONOMISTS: FELLOWS

Richard M. Alt
Agency for Int. Development

William F. Butler
Chase Manhattan Bank

Elmer C. Bratt
Lehigh University

William P. Carlin
Republic Steel Corporation

Arthur Brickner
Bankers Trust Company

William H. Chartener
U.S. Department of Commerce

Ralph E. Burgess
Natl. Assn. of Securities Dlrs.

William A. Clark
Monsanto Company

Donald R. Burris
Texas Instruments Inc.

Richard W. Clemence
Wellesley College

James M. Dawson
National City Bk. of Cleveland

Joel Dean
Joel Dean Associates

Ira T. Ellis
E. I. Du Pont de Nemours & Co.

Richard W. Everett
Chase Manhattan Bank

Alan Greenspan
Townsend Greenspan & Co.

Walter Hoadley
Bank of America NT & SA

George W. James
Air Transport Assoc. of Amer.

Herbert E. Johnson
Cont. Ill. Natl. Bank & Trust Co.

Dexter M. Keezer
(Retired)

Lester S. Kellogg
(Retired)

Irving Lipkowitz
Reynolds Metals Company

Joseph A. Livingston
Philadelphia Bulletin

George W. McKinney, Jr.
Irving Trust Company

Stanley V. Malcuit
Aluminum Co. of America

A. James Meigs
First National City Bank

David C. Melnicoff
Federal Reserve Bk. of Phila.

Edmund A. Mennis
Republic Natl. Bank of Dallas

M. Dutton Morehouse
Brown Bros. Harriman & Company

Sanford Parker
Fortune Magazine

Harrold Passer
U.S. Dept. of Commerce

Sidney E. Rolfe
Agora Development Corporation

Arthur Rosenbaum
(Retired)

William H. Shaw
E. I. Du Pont de Nemours & Co.

Charles E. Silberman
Fortune Magazine

Myron S. Silbert
Lehman Brothers

Leonard Silk
Brookings Institution

George Cline Smith
MacKay-Shields Economics, Inc.

Albert T. Sommers
National Ind. Conf. Board

Herbert Stein
Council of Economic Advisers

George W. Terborgh
Machinery & Allied Products

William W. Tongue
University of Chicago

Robert P. Ulin
Mobil Oil Corporation

Willis Winn
Wharton School, University of
  Pennsylvania

Robert D. Woodward
Bethlehem Steel Corporation

Wilson Wright
(Retired)

"On the Hill and Downtown"

Any roster of living and influential economists in government would, of course, include members of the Council of Economic Advisers, the Joint Committee staff, the White House advisers, the Federal Reserve System, and the executive agencies. Such a list might include:

Gardner Ackley (CEA, White House)
Louis Bean (USDA)
Ewan Clague (Bureau of Labor Statistics)
Grover Ensley (JEC)
Mordecai Ezekiel (USDA)
Herbert Feis (State Dept.)
Richard V. Gilbert (Commerce)
Gabriel Hauge (White House)
Walter W. Heller (CEA)
Leon Keyserling (CEA)
James Knowles (JEC)
Paul McCracken (CEA)
Sherman Maisel (Federal Reserve System)
Edwin G. Nourse (CEA)
Arthur Okun (CEA)
Robert V. Roosa (Treasury)
Dan T. Smith (Treasury)
Arthur Smithies (Bureau of the Budget)
Woodlief Thomas (Federal Reserve System)
Willard Thorp (State Dept.)
James Tobin (CEA)
Rexford G. Tugwell (USDA, White House)
Ralph Young (Federal Reserve System)

APPENDIX B
Typical U.S. Firms
Employing Professional Economists

The following U.S. firms are typical of those employing professional economists.

Aetna Life Affiliated Cos.
Air Reduction Company, Inc.
Allegheny Ludlum Steel Corp.
Allied Chemical Corp.
Allis-Chalmers Mfg. Co.
Aluminum Company of America
American Airlines, Inc.
American Can Co.
American Metals Climax, Inc.
American Motors Corp.
American Tel. & Tel. Co.
American Viscose Corp.
Anderson, Clayton & Co.
Anheuser-Busch, Inc.
Arabian American Oil Co.
Armstrong Cork Co.
Ashland Oil & Refining Co.
Atchison, Topeka & Santa Fe
  Railway Co.
Atlantic Richfield Co.
Auchincloss Parker & Redpath
Bache & Co.
Bank of California
Bank of New York
The Bank of Virginia
R. L. Banks & Associates, Inc.

Batton, Barton, Durstine & Osborn
Bechtel Corp.
The Bell Telephone Co. of Pa.
Bethlehem Steel Corp.
The Boeing Company
Booz, Allen & Hamilton, Inc.
Borg Warner Corp.—Norge Div.
Braniff International
Bristol-Myers Co.
British American Oil Co., Ltd.
Brown Brothers Harriman & Co.
The Budd Company
Burroughs Corp.
Business Week
Campbell Soup Co.
Carling Brewing Co.
Carrier Air Conditioning Co.
Caterpillar Tractor Co.
Celanese Fibers Mktg. Co.
Chase Manhattan Bank
Chemical Bank N.Y. Trust Co.
Chesapeake & Ohio Railway Co.
Chesapeake & Potomac Tel. Cos.
Chicago & Northwestern Rwy. Co.
Chris Craft Corp.
Chrysler Motors Corp.

Ciba Corp.
Clark Equipment Co.
Cleveland-Cliff Iron Co.
Cleveland Elec. Illuminating Co.
Columbia Broadcasting System
Combustion Engineering, Inc.
Communications Satellite Corp.
The Connecticut Bank & Trust Co.
Continental Can Co., Inc.
Continental Illinois National Bank
  & Trust Co.
Continental Motors Corp.
Continental Oil Co.
Crocker-Citizens Natl. Bank
Cresap, McCormick & Paget
Crucible Steel Co. of America
Cummins Engine Co., Inc.
Curtis Publishing Co.
Deere & Company
Deering, Milliken Corp.
Detroit Bank & Trust Co.
Detroit Edison Co.
The Dow Chemical Co.
E. I. Du Pont de Nemours & Co.
Eastern Air Lines, Inc.
Eastman Dillon, Union Securities
  & Company
Eastman Kodak Co.
Eaton, Yale & Towne, Inc.
Emerson Electric Co.
Equitable Life Assur. Society of
  U.S.
Esso Chemical Co., Inc.
Federated Dept. Stores, Inc.
First National Bank of Atlanta
First National Bank of Chicago
First National City Bank (N.Y.)
Ford Motor Company
Foremost Dairies, Inc.
Formica Corp.
General Aniline & Film Corp.
General Electric Co.
General Foods Corp.

General Motors Corp.
General Telephone & Electronics
  Corp.
Getty Oil Co.
Girard Trust Bank
The Glidden Co.
Goldman, Sachs & Co.
Goodbody & Company
B. F. Goodrich Co.
W. R. Grace & Co.
Gulf Oil Co.
Harris Trust & Savings Bank
Honeywell, Inc.
Hooker Chemical Corp.
Hughes Tool Co.
Humble Oil & Refining Co.
E. F. Hutton & Co., Inc.
Illinois Bell Telephone Co.
Inland Steel Co.
IBM Corp.
International Harvester Co.
International Nickel Company, Inc.
Investors Diversified Services
Irving Trust Co.
John Hancock Mutual Life Ins. Co.
Johns-Manville Co.
Johnson & Johnson
Kaiser Aluminum & Chem. Sales,
  Inc.
Kaiser Industries Corp.
Kimberly Clark Corp.
Koppers Co., Inc.
Lear Siegler, Inc.
Lehman Brothers
Eli Lilly & Co.
Link-Belt Div. FMC Corp.
Massachusetts Investors Trust
McGraw-Hill, Inc.
The Mead Corp.
Mellon National Bank & Trust Co.
Merck & Company, Inc.
Merrill Lynch-Pierce-Fenner &
  Smith

Metropolitan Life Ins. Co.
National Cash Register Co.
Mobil Oil Corp.
Monsanto Co.
Montgomery Ward
Morgan Guaranty Trust Co.
 (N.Y.)
National Gypsum Co.
New York Life Insurance Co.
New York Stock Exchange
New York Telephone Co.
North American Aviation, Inc.
North Carolina National Bank
Northern Illinois Gas Co.
Northrop Corp.
Ohio Brass Co.
Olin Mathieson Chemical Corp.
Olivetti Underwood Corp.
Otis Elevator Co.
Owens-Corning Fiberglas Corp.
Owens-Illinois, Inc.
Pacific Gas & Electric Co.
J. C. Penney
Pennsylvania Power & Light Co.
Penn-Central Transportation Co.
Pfizer, Charles & Co.
Philco-Ford Corp.
Phillips Petroleum Co.
Piper Aircraft Corp.
PPG Industries
Procter & Gamble Co.
Prudential Ins. Co. of America
Pullman-Standard
Quaker Oats Co.
Radio Corp. of America
Ralston Purina Co.
Raybestos-Manhattan, Inc.
Raytheon Co.
Republic National Bank of Dallas
Republic Steel Corp.

Reynolds Metals Co.
Rockwell-Standard
Safeway Stores, Inc.
St. Regis Paper Co.
Schenley Industries, Inc.
Scott Paper Co.
Shell Chemical Co.
Shell Oil Co.
Shell Pipeline Corp.
Signal Oil & Gas Co.
SKF Industries, Inc.
Smith Kline & French Lab.
Southern Railway System
Sperry Rand Corp.
Standard Oil Co. of N.J.
J. P. Stevens & Co., Inc.
Sun Oil Co.
Swift & Co.
Texas Eastern Transmission Corp.
Texas Instruments, Inc.
Trans World Airlines, Inc.
T R W, Inc.
Union Carbide Corp.
Union Oil Co. of California
Union Pacific Railroad Co.
Union Tank Car Company
United Aircraft Corp.
United Air Lines
United Shoe Machinery Corp.
U.S. Steel Corp.
Vulcan Materials Co.
Wachovia Bank & Trust Co.
West Virginia Pulp & Paper
Western Air Lines, Inc.
Western Electric Co.
Western Pacific Railroad Co.
Worthington Corp.
Westinghouse Electric Corp.
Weyerhaeuser Co.

Bibliography

Acheson, Dean G. *Present at the Creation*. New York: W. W. Norton & Co., 1969.

Ackley, Gardner. "Contribution of Economists to Policy Formulation," *Journal of Finance*, Vol. XXI, No. 2 (May, 1966), pp. 170ff.

Adams, Sherman. *First Hand Report*. New York: Harper and Row, 1961.

Alexander, K. J. W.; A. G. Kemp; and T. M. Rybezynski, eds. *The Economist in Business*. New York: Augustus M. Kelley, 1967.

American Economic Association. *AEA Handbook*. Evanston: American Economic Association, 1969.

Anderson, Patrick. *The President's Men*. Garden City: Doubleday and Co., Inc., 1968.

Arthur, Henry B. "Help from the Company Economist," *Harvard Business Review* (September–October, 1961), pp. 10–27.

Ayres, C. E. *The Industrial Economy*. Boston: Houghton Mifflin Co., 1952.

Bach, George. *Economics*. Englewood Cliffs, N.J.: Prentice-Hall, Inc., 1966.

Bailey, Stephen Kemp. *Congress Makes a Law*. New York: Columbia University Press, 1950.

Baran, Paul. "National Economic Planning," in *A Survey of Contemporary Economics*. Ed. by Bernard F. Haley. Vol. 2. American Economic Association. Homewood, Ill.: Richard D. Irwin, 1952.

Barzun, Jacques. *The American University*. New York: Harper and Row, 1968.

Becker, Gary S. *The Economics of Discrimination.* Chicago: University of Chicago Press, 1957.

Bernstein, Marver H. *Regulating Business by Independent Regulatory Commission.* Princeton: Princeton University Press, 1955.

Blair, John M. "Lawyers and Economists in Antitrust: A Marriage of Necessity If Not Convenience," *Proceedings,* American Bar Association, Vols. 20–23, 1962–63 (April, 1962), pp. 29–37.

Boddy, Francis M. "Recent Behavior of Economists' Salaries," *American Economic Review,* Papers and Proceedings, Eighty-second Annual Meeting, American Economic Association, Vol. LXI, No. 2 (May, 1970), pp. 343–50.

Boulding, Kenneth L. "Is Economics Culture Bound?" *American Economic Review,* Papers and Proceedings, Eighty-second Annual Meeting, American Economic Association, Vol. LXI, No. 2 (May, 1970), pp. 406–12.

———. "Presidential Address, American Economic Association, 1969," *American Economic Review,* Vol. LIX, No. 1 (March, 1969), pp. 1–12.

———. *Principles of Economic Policy.* Englewood Cliffs, N.J.: Prentice-Hall, Inc., 1958.

Bowen, Howard. "Graduate Education in Economics," *American Economic Review,* Supplement, Vol. XLIII, No. 4, Pt. 2 (September, 1953).

Bratt, Elmer G., and Milton G. Grannatt, Jr. "Survey of Business Economists," *Business Economics* (September, 1970), pp. 41–48.

Breit, William, and Roger L. Ransom. *The Academic Scribblers.* New York: Holt, Rinehart and Winston, 1971.

Brimmer, Andrew, and Harriett Harper. "Economists' Perception of Minority Economic Problems: A View of Emerging Literature," *Journal of Economic Literature,* Vol. VIII, No. 3 (September, 1970), pp. 783–805.

Bronfenbrenner, Martin. "Radical Economics in America," *Journal of Economic Literature,* Vol. VIII, No. 3 (September, 1970), pp. 747–67.

———. "Trends, Cycles, and Fads in Economic Writing," *American Economic Review,* Vol. LV, No. 2 (May, 1966), pp. 538–52.

Burns, Arthur F. "An Economist in Government," *Forum I* (Winter, 1957).

———. *The Management of Prosperity.* Pittsburgh: Carnegie Institute of Technology, 1966.

Butler, William F., and Robert A. Karesh, eds. *How Business Economists Forecast.* Englewood Cliffs, N.J.: Prentice-Hall, Inc., 1966.

Canterbery, E. Ray. "The Diminishing Uselessness of Economists in Business, *Mississippi Valley Journal of Business and Economics,* Vol. I, No. 1 (Fall, 1965), pp. 1–13.

———. *Economics on a New Frontier.* Belmont: Wadsworth Publishing Co., 1968.

———. *The President's Council of Economic Advisers.* New York: Exposition Press, 1961.

Caplow, Theodore, and Reece J. McGee. *The Academic Marketplace.* New York: Basic Books Inc., 1958.

Carincross, Alec K. "Economists in Government," *Lloyds Bank Review,* No. 95 (January, 1970), pp. 1–18.

———. "On Being an Economic Advisor," *Scottish Journal of Political Economy,* No. 2 (October, 1955), pp. 181–97.

Cartter, Allan. *An Assessment of Quality in Graduate Education.* Washington, D.C.: American Council on Education, 1966.

Chandler, Cleveland A. "An Affirmative Action Plan for the Economics Profession," *American Economic Review,* Papers and Proceedings, Eighty-second Annual Meeting, American Economic Association, Vol. LXI, No. 2 (May, 1970), pp. 412–26.

Clague, Ewan. "The Supply of Economists," *American Economic Review,* Vol. LII, No. 2 (May, 1962), pp. 497ff.

Coats, A. W. "The American Political Economy Club," *American Economic Review,* Vol. LI (September, 1961), pp. 624–37.

Cochran, Thomas C. *Railroad Leaders, 1845–1890.* Cambridge, Mass.: Harvard University Press, 1953.

Colm, Gerhard. *Essays in Public Finance and Fiscal Policy.* New York: Oxford University Press, 1955.

———. Letter to Gert von Eynern. *Interdependensen von Politik and Wirtshaft.* Berlin: Festgabe fur Gert von Eynern, Duncker and Humbolt, July, 1966.

Committee on the National Science Foundation Report in the Economics Profession. "Structure of Economists' Employment and Salaries, 1964," *American Economic Review,* Vol. LV, No. 4, Pt. 2 (December, 1965).

Dean, Joel. *Managerial Economics.* Englewood Cliffs, N.J.: Prentice-Hall, Inc., 1951.

Dernburg, Thomas F., and Duncan M. McDougall. *Macroeconomics.* McGraw-Hill Book Co., 1960.

Devons, Ely. "The Role of the Economist in Public Affairs," *Lloyds Bank Review,* No. 53 (July, 1959), pp. 26–38.

Dillard, Dudley. *The Economics of John Maynard Keynes.* Englewood Cliffs, N.J.: Prentice-Hall, Inc., 1946.

Donhoff, G. William. *The Higher Circles.* New York: Random House, Inc., 1970.

Dorfman, Joseph. "The Department of Economics," in *A History of the Faculty of Political Science.* New York: Columbia University Press, 1955.

―――. *The Economic Mind in American Civilization.* New York: Viking Press, 1949.

―――. *Thorstein Veblen and His America.* New York: Viking Press, 1934.

"Economics in the Schools" (a committee report), *American Economic Review,* American Economic Association Supplement, Vol. LIII, No. 1, Pt. 2 (March, 1963).

"Economists Consider Economic Reporters and Vice Versa" (a panel discussion), *Proceedings,* American Economic Association, Vol. LXII, No. 2 (May, 1972).

Edwards, Richard C., *et al.* "A Radical Approach to Economics: Basis for a New Curriculum," *American Economic Review,* Papers and Proceedings, Eighty-second Annual Meeting, American Economic Association, Vol. LXI, No. 2 (May, 1970).

Federal Reserve Bank of Boston. "The 7-Year Lag: The Market for Economists," *New England Business Review* (December, 1964), pp. 1–9.

Ferber, Robert, and P. J. Verdoorn. *Research Methods in Economics and Business.* New York: Macmillan Co., 1962.

Fine, Sidney. *Laissez-Faire and the General Welfare State.* Ann Arbor: University of Michigan Press, 1964.

Flash, Edward S. *Economic Advice and Presidential Leadership.* New York: Columbia University Press, 1965.

Friedman, Milton. *Capitalism and Freedom.* Chicago: University of Chicago Press, 1962.

―――. *Essays in Positive Economics.* Chicago: University of Chicago Press, 1953.

Frisch, Ragnar. *Theory of Production.* Dordrech-Holland: D. Reidel Publishing Co.; and Chicago: Rand McNally and Co., 1965.

Fusfeld, Daniel. *The Age of the Economist.* Glenview, Ill.: Scott Foresman & Co., 1966.

―――. *The Economic Thought of Franklin Roosevelt and the Origins of the New Deal.* New York: Columbia University Press, 1956.

Galbraith, John Kenneth. *The Affluent Society*. Boston: Houghton Mifflin Co., 1958.

———. *American Capitalism: The Concept of Countervailing Power*. Boston: Houghton Mifflin Co., 1952.

———. *Economics and the Art of Controversy*. New Brunswick: Rutgers University Press, 1955.

———. *Economics, Peace and Laughter*. Boston: Houghton Mifflin Co., 1971.

———. *The Liberal Hour*. Boston: Houghton Mifflin Co., 1960.

———. *The New Industrial State*. New York: Signet Books, New American Library, Inc., 1968.

Gordon, Robert A., and James E. Howell. *Higher Education for Business*. New York: Columbia University Press, 1959.

Gordon, S. D. "Attitudes Toward Trusts Prior to the Sherman Act," *Southern Economic Journal*, Vol. XXX (October, 1966), pp. 160–81.

Gruchy, Allan G. *Modern Economic Thought*. Englewood Cliffs, N.J.: Prentice-Hall, Inc., 1947.

Hall, Robert. *The Place of the Economist in Government*. Oxford Economic Papers, No. 7 (June, 1955), pp. 119–35.

Hallett, Graham. "The Role of Economists as Government Advisors," *Westminster Bank Review* (May, 1967), pp. 67–81.

Hansen, Alvin. *The American Economy*. New York: McGraw-Hill Book Co., 1957.

———. *Business Cycles and National Income*. New York: W. W. Norton & Co., 1964.

———. *Economic Issues in the 1960's*. New York: McGraw-Hill Book Co., 1960.

———. *Economic Policy and Full Employment*. New York: McGraw-Hill Book Co., 1947.

———. "Keynes After Thirty Years (With Reference to the United States)." *Weltwirtshaftlicher Archives*, Band 97, Heftz, 1966, pp. 15–27.

Harrington Michael. *The Accidental Century*. New York: Macmillan Co., 1965.

Harris, Seymour E. *Economics of the Kennedy Years*. New York: Harper and Row, 1964.

———. *The New Economics*. New York: Alfred A. Knopf, Inc., 1957.

———, ed. *Saving America's Capitalism*. New York: Alfred A. Knopf, Inc., 1948.

Harrod, Roy. *Economic Essays*. New York: Harcourt, Brace and World, 1952.

———. *Life of John Maynard Keynes*. New York: Harcourt, Brace and World, 1951.

Hayek, Frederick A. *The Road to Serfdom*. Chicago: University of Chicago Press, 1944.

Heilbroner, Robert L. *The Making of Economic Society*. Englewood Cliffs, N.J.: Prentice-Hall, Inc., 1962.

Heller, Walter W. *New Dimensions in Political Economy*. Cambridge, Mass.: Harvard University Press, 1966.

Henderson, P. D. *The Use of Economists in British Administration*. Oxford Economic Papers, No. 13 (February, 1961), pp. 5–26.

Hitch, Charles J. *The Uses of Economics*. Santa Monica: Rand Corporation, 1960.

Hoadley, Walter E. "Ethical Problems of the Economist in His Firm," *Business Economics*, Vol. II, No. 1 (Fall, 1956), pp. 10–17.

Hoover, Calvin B. *The Economy, Liberty and the State*. New York: Twentieth Century Fund, 1959.

Hutchinson, T. W. *Economics and Economic Policy in Britain, 1946–66*. London: Allen and Unwin, 1968.

———. *The Significance and Basic Postulates of Economic Theory*. New York: Augustus M. Kelley, 1960.

Janeway, Eliot. *The Economics of Crisis*. New York: Weybright and Tally, Inc., 1968.

Jewkes, John. *Ordeal by Planning*. New York: Macmillan Co., 1948.

Johnson, Herbert E. "Presidential Address to the National Association of Business Economists." Chicago, 25 September 1969.

Josephson, Matthew and Hanah. *Al Smith: Hero of the Cities*. Boston: Houghton Mifflin Co., 1969.

Keynes, J. M. *Essays in Biography*. London: Macmillan Co. Ltd., 1933.

Kiker, B. F., and Robert J. Carlsson, eds. *South Carolina Economists: Essays on the Evolution of Antebellum Thought*. Essays in Economics Series, Vol. 20. Columbia: University of South Carolina Bureau of Business and Economic Research, 1969.

Kirk, Russell. *The Conservative Mind*. Chicago: Regency Press, 1953.

Kirzner, Israel. *The Economic Point of View*. New York: D. Van Nostrand Co., 1960.

Knight, Frank H. *The Ethics of Competition*. New York: Harper and Row, 1935.

————. "The Nature of Economic Science in Some Recent Discussion," *American Economic Review,* Vol. XXIV, No. 2 (June, 1934), pp. 1–19.

Koopmans, Tjalling C. *Three Essays on the State of Economic Science.* New York: McGraw-Hill Book Co., 1957.

Krock, Arthur. *Memoirs: Sixty Years on the Firing Line.* New York: Funk and Wagnalls, 1968.

Krupp, Sherman Roy, ed. *The Structure of Economic Science.* Englewood Cliffs, N.J.: Prentice-Hall, Inc., 1966.

Lancaster, Kelvin. *Mathematical Economics.* New York: Macmillan Co., 1968.

Leamer, Laurence E. "A Brief History of Economics in General Education," *American Economic Review,* Teaching Undergraduate Economics, Vol. XL, No. 5 (December, 1950), pp. 16–26.

Lekachman, Robert. *The Age of Keynes.* New York: Random House, Vintage Books, 1968.

————. *A History of Economic Ideas.* New York: Harper and Row, 1959.

————. "The Quarrelsome Economists," *New Leader,* 13 October 1969.

Lerner, Max, ed. *The Portable Veblen.* New York: Viking Press, 1948.

Lippman, Walter. *The Good Society.* New York: Grosset and Dunlap, 1934.

Little, J. M. D. "The Economist in Whitehall," *Lloyds Bank Review,* No. 44 (April, 1957), pp. 29–40.

Lutrell, W. F. "The Work of an Economic Consultant: The Economist in Business," in *The Economist in Business.* Ed. by K. J. W. Alexander, A. G. Kemp, and T. M. Rybezynski. New York: Augustus M. Kelly, 1967.

McCloskey, Robert G. *The American Supreme Court.* Chicago: University of Chicago Press, 1960.

Makhlup, Fritz. *The Political Economy of Monopoly.* Baltimore: Johns Hopkins University Press, 1964.

Max, Peter. "Economics in the Courtroom," *Antitrust Law and Economics Review,* Vol. I, No. 4 (Summer, 1968), pp. 47–69.

Maxwell, W. David. *Price Theory and Applications in Business Administration.* Pacific Palisades: Goodyear Publishing Co., 1970.

Mill, John Stuart. *Essays on Some Unsettled Questions of Political Economy.* London: Macmillan Co. Ltd., 1844.

Mitchell, Broadus. *Depression Decade.* New York: Holt, Rinehart and Winston, 1961.

Morgenstern, Oskar. *The Limits of Economics*. London: Wm. Hodge & Co., Ltd., 1937.

Morin, Alexander. "The Market for Professional Writing in Economics," *American Economic Review*, Vol. LVI, No. 1 (March, 1966), pp. 287–334.

National Association of Business Economists. *Business Economics Careers*. Washington, D.C.: National Association of Business Economists, 1968.

National Science Foundation. *National Register of Scientific Personnel*. Washington, D.C.: National Science Foundation, 1970.

————. *Summary of American Science Manpower*. Washington, D.C.: National Science Foundation, 1970.

New York Times, 27 October 1970, p. 67.

New York Times, "Worldly Prophets," 27 December 1970, Sec. 3, p. 1.

Norton, Hugh S. *Economic Policy: Government and Business*. Columbus: Charles E. Merrill Publishing Co., 1966.

————. *The Professional Economist: His Role in Business and Industry*. Essays in Economics Series, Vol. 19. Columbia: University of South Carolina Bureau of Business and Economic Research, 1969.

————. *The Role of the Economist in Government Policy Making*. Berkeley: McCutchan Publishing Corp., 1969.

Nourse, Edwin G. *Economics in the Public Service*. New York: Harcourt, Brace, & World, 1955.

Nourse to Norton (letter), 23 December 1969.

O'Connor, Michael J. L. *Origins of Academic Economics in the United States*. New York: Columbia University Press, 1944.

Okun, Arthur M. *The Battle Against Unemployment*. New York: W. W. Norton & Co., 1965.

————. *The Political Economy of Prosperity*. Washington, D.C.: Brookings Institution, 1971.

Parrish, John B. "Rise of Economics as an Academic Discipline: The Formative Years," *Southern Economic Journal*, Vol. XXXIV, No. 1 (July, 1967), pp. 2–16.

Pigou, A. C. *Memorials to Alfred Marshall*. London: Macmillan Co. Ltd., 1925.

Radom, Matthew. *The Social Scientists in American Industry*. New Brunswick: Rutgers University Press, 1971.

Robbins, Lionel. *Autobiography of an Economist*. London: Macmillan Co. Ltd., 1971.

————. *The Economist in the Twentieth Century*. London: Macmillan Co. Ltd., 1954.

————. *The Nature and Significance of Economic Science*. London: Macmillan Co. Ltd., 1948.

Robinson, Colin. "Economic Forecasting in the Esso Petroleum Co., Ltd.," in *The Economist in Business*. Ed. by K. J. W. Alexander, A. G. Kemp, and T. M. Rybezynski. New York: Augustus M. Kelley, 1967.

Robinson, Colin, *et al. An Introduction to Economic Reasoning*. Washington, D.C.: Brookings Institution, 1956.

Rodell, Fred. *Nine Men*. New York: Random House, Inc., 1955.

Roll, Eric. *History of Economic Thought*. Englewood Cliffs, N.J.: Prentice-Hall, Inc., 1947.

Romano, R., and M. Leiman, eds. *Views of Capitalism*. Beverly Hills: Free Press of Glencoe, 1970.

Rosenman, Samuel I. *Working with Roosevelt*. New York: Harper and Row, 1952.

Rossant, M. J. "Ethics in the Age of the Economist," *Business Economics*, Vol. II, No. 1 (Fall, 1956), pp. 20–24.

Rossiter, Clinton. *Conservatism in America*. New York: Alfred A. Knopf, Inc., 1955.

"Round Table Session on the Academic Labor Market," *American Economic Review, Papers and Proceedings*, Vol. XLI, No. 2 (May, 1971).

Ruggles, Nancy, ed. *Economics. Behavioral and Social Sciences Survey*. Englewood Cliffs, N.J.: Prentice-Hall, Inc., 1970.

Rummel, J. Francis, and Wesley C. Ballaine. *Research Methods in Business*. New York: Harper and Row, 1963.

Samuelson, Paul A. *Economics*. New York: McGraw-Hill Book Co., 1971.

————. "Economists and the History of Ideas," *American Economic Review*, Vol. LII, No. 1 (March, 1962), pp. 1–18.

Saulnier, Raymond J. *The Strategy of Economic Policy*. New York: Fordham University Press, 1962.

Saunders, Charles B. *The Brookings Institution: A Fifty Year History*. Washington, D.C.: Brookings Institution, 1966.

Schelling, Thomas C. *National Income Behavior*. New York: McGraw-Hill Book Co., 1951.

Schlesinger, Arthur. *The Age of Roosevelt: The Politics of Upheaval*. Vol. 3. Boston: Houghton Mifflin Co., 1953.

Schriftgiesser, Karl. *Business and Economic Policy: The Role of the*

Committee for Economic Development, 1942–1967. Englewood Cliffs, N.J.: Prentice-Hall, Inc., 1967.

Schultze, Charles L. *National Income Analysis*. Englewood Cliffs, N.J.: Prentice-Hall, Inc., 1964.

Schumpeter, Joseph A. *History of Economic Analysis*. New York: Oxford University Press, 1954.

———. *Ten Great Economists*. New York: Oxford University Press, 1951.

Seligman, Ben B. *Main Currents in Modern Economics: Economic Thought Since 1870*. Beverly Hills: Free Press of Glencoe, 1962.

Sievers, Allen M. *Revolution and the Economic Order*. Englewood Cliffs, N.J.: Prentice-Hall, Inc., 1962.

Silberman, Charles, and Sanford S. Parker. "The Economy's Scouts," *Fortune*, Vol. 52, No. 6 (December, 1955), pp. 100–103ff.

Silk, Leonard S. "The Business Economist and the Academic Economist." Paper delivered 13 November 1969 to the Thirty-ninth Annual Conference of the Southern Economic Association, St. Louis. Mimeographed.

Silverman, Corrine. *The President's Council of Economic Advisers*. Inter-University Case Program, No. 48. Indianapolis: Boggs-Merrill Co., 1959.

Simons, Henry C. *Economic Policy for a Free Society*. Chicago: University of Chicago Press, 1948.

Solow, Robert M. "The New Industrial State, Son of Affluence," *Public Interest*, Vol. 9 (Fall, 1967), pp. 100–108.

Somers, Gerald G. "The Functioning Market for Economists," *American Economic Review*, Papers and Proceedings, Vol. XLI, No. 2 (May, 1971).

Sorensen, Theodore C. *Kennedy*. New York: Harper and Row, Bantam Ed., 1966.

Spencer, Milton H., and Louis Siegelman. *Managerial Economics*. Homewood, Ill.: Richard D. Irwin, 1959.

Spengler, Joseph J. "Economics: Its History, Themes, and Approaches," *Journal of Economic Issues*, Vol. 12 (March, 1968), pp. 116–37.

Spiegel, Henry W. *Current Economic Problems*. Homewood, Ill.: Richard D. Irwin, 1961.

Stein, Herbert. *The Fiscal Revolution in America*. Chicago: University of Chicago Graduate School of Business, 1969.

Sternsher, Bernard. *Rexford G. Tugwell and the New Deal*. New Brunswick: Rutgers University Press, 1956.

Stigler, George J. "The Economist and the State," *American Economic Review*, Vol. LV, No. 1 (March, 1965), pp. 1–12.

———. *Essays in the History of Economics*. Chicago: University of Chicago Press, 1965.

———. *The Intellectual and the Marketplace*. Beverly Hills: Free Press of Glencoe, 1963.

Sutton, Francis X., *et al. The American Business Creed*. Cambridge, Mass.: Harvard University Press, 1956.

Sweezy, Alan R. "The Keynesian Revolution and Its Pioneers," *Proceedings*, American Economic Association, Vol. LVII, No. 2 (May, 1972).

Tanzer, Lester, ed. *The Kennedy Circle*. Washington, D.C.: Luce, 1961.

Teitsworth, Clark. "The Growing Role of the Company Economist," *Harvard Business Review*, Vol. 37, No. 1 (January–February, 1959), pp. 97–104.

Terbrough, George. "Ethics of Advocacy," *Business Economics*, Vol. II, No. 1 (Fall, 1956), pp. 14–20.

Thurow, Lester C. *Poverty and Discrimination*. Washington, D.C.: Brookings Institution, 1960.

Time, 19 December 1969.

Tobin, James. "The Intellectual Revolution in U.S. Economic Policy Making." Noel Buxton Lecture, 18 January 1966, at the University of Essex. Mimeographed.

———. *National Economic Policy*. New Haven: Yale University Press, 1966.

Tolles, N. Arnold, and Emanuel Melchar. "Studies of the Structure of Economists' Salaries and Income," *American Economic Review*, Supplement, Vol. LVIII, No. 5, pt. 2 (December, 1968).

Tugwell, Rexford G. *The Brains Trust*. New York: Viking Press, 1968.

Tullock, Gordon. *The Organization of Inquiry*. Durham: Duke University Press, 1966.

U.S. Bureau of Manpower Information Systems. *Occupations of Federal White Collar Workers*. USCC Statement SM–56–7. Washington, D.C.: Government Printing Office, 1967.

U.S. Congress. *Congressional Directory*. 91st Cong. Washington, D.C.: Government Printing Office, March, 1969.

U.S. Congress, Joint Economic Committee. "Twentieth Anniversary of the Employment Act of 1946," *An Economic Symposium*. 89th Cong., 2nd sess. Washington, D.C.: Government Printing Office, 1966.

U.S. Congress, Subcommittee on General Credit Control and Debt Management. *Monetary Policy and the Public Debt Hearings.* 82nd Cong. Washington, D.C.: Government Printing Office, March, 1952.

U.S. President. *The Economic Report of the President.* Washington, D.C.: Government Printing Office, February, 1970.

Von Mises, Ludwig. *Human Action.* New Haven: Yale University Press, 1949.

Walsh, Vivian Charles. *Introduction to Contemporary Microeconomics.* New York: McGraw-Hill Book Co., 1970.

Wasserman, Paul, and Willis P. Greer. *Consultants and Consulting Organizations.* Ithaca: Cornell University Graduate School of Business and Public Administration, 1969.

Watson, D. S. *Economic Policy: Business and Government.* Boston: Houghton Mifflin Co., 1960.

Weaver, James H. "Toward a Radical Political Economics," *American Economist,* Vol. XIV, No. 1 (Spring, 1970), pp. 1–11.

Weiss, Leonard W. *Case Studies in American Industry.* New York: John Wiley & Sons, Inc., 1967.

White, Theodore H. "The Action Intellectuals," *Life,* 9 June 1967.

Wilcox, Clair. *Public Policies Toward Business.* Homewood, Ill.: Richard D. Irwin, 1960.

Wilkins, B. H., and C. B. Friday, eds. *The Economists of the New Frontier.* New York: Random House, Inc., 1963.

Wright, David McCord. *Democracy and Progress.* New York: Macmillan Co., 1948.

Wright, Wilson. *Forecasting for Profit.* New York: John Wiley & Sons, Inc., 1947.

Zweig, Michael. *A New Left Critique of Radical Economics.* Ann Arbor: Union for Radical Political Economics, 1969.

Index

Index

Abromovitz, Moses, 141
Academic economists and: consulting, 47, 48; writing, 48, 49
Academic writing, financial rewards of, 49
Acheson, Dean G., 132n
Ackley, Gardner, 77, 78, 99
Adams, Sherman, 91, 92n
Agricultural economists, 84, 84n
Alexander, K. J. W., 109n
Alt, Richard M., 143
Amateur economists, 4n, 5
American Association of Graduate Schools, 26
American Association of University Professors, 56n
American Economist, 29n
American Economic Association, 14, 55, 61, 62
American Economic Review, 13n, 23, 29n, 56, 56n
Anderson, Patrick, 74, 74n
Anti-Trust Law and Economics Review, 24
Armstrong Cork Co., 110
Arrow, Kenneth J., 62, 141
Awards to economists: Abramson

Award, 63n; John Bates Clark Medal, 62; Nobel Prize, 62, 63; Francis A. Walker Medal, 62
Ayres, C. E., 30, 30n

Bach, George, 18n
Bachelors degrees in economics, and other fields, 53
Bain, Joe S., 141
Baran, Paul, 35
Barzun, Jacques, 42n
Baumol, William J., 141
Bean, Louis, 145
Becker, Gary S., 11n, 62, 141
Bernstein, Marver, 86n
Black economists, 11–12, 11n
Blair, John M., 88n
Board of Economic Warfare, 106
Boulding, Kenneth, 61, 61n, 62, 135n, 136, 137, 141
Bowen, Howard, 54n
"Brains Trust," in "New Deal," 72, 73, 73n
Bratt, Elmer C., 118n, 143
Breit, William, 61n
Brickner, Arthur, 143

163

*The World
of the Economist*

Composed in Linotype Bodoni Book by Kingsport Press
with selected lines of display in Scotch Roman. Printed
letterpress by Kingsport Press on Warren's University
Text, an acid-free paper noted for its longevity. The paper
was expressly watermarked for the University of South
Carolina Press with the Press colophon. Binding by
Kingsport Press in Holliston's Kingston natural finish
fabric over .088 boards. Designed by Bill Crittendon.

 UNIVERSITY OF SOUTH CAROLINA PRESS
Columbia, South Carolina